Praise for the *Letters to My Younger Self* series

"Ingenious . . . the rare self-help volume that young women would elect to read and decidedly enjoy."
—*Publishers Weekly*

"*What I Know About Success* is a good read for the bad times and makes a great gift for the graduating teenager who may need advice, looking back."
—*Bookworm Sez*

"*If I'd Known Then* contains inspirational advice for young women from the people who know them best: themselves . . . their advice applies to everyday, ordinary women—at any stage of life."
—*Fredericksburg Free-Lance Star*

"With candid discussions of body image, alcoholism, death, insecurity and trying to succeed in the face of seemingly impossible circumstances, this is a great conversation starter for girls."
—*Style Weekly*

"It's hard not to relate to these letters on one level or another. Who hasn't felt loss or disappointment? Readers will leave *If I'd Known Then* inspired to look back on their own lives and write their own missive to themselves."
—*Deseret Morning News*

ALSO EDITED BY ELLYN SPRAGINS

*If I'd Known Then: Women in Their 20s and 30s
Write Letters to Their Younger Selves*

What I Know Now: Letters to My Younger Self

WHAT I KNOW NOW ABOUT SUCCESS

Letters from
Extraordinary Women to
Their Younger Selves

Edited by
ELLYN SPRAGINS

Da Capo
LIFE
LONG

A Member of the Perseus Books Group

For my mother, Joyce Dingley Spragins,
a gorgeous spirit.

Copyright © 2010 by Ellyn Spragins

Set in 11 point Adobe Caslon by the Perseus Books Group

Cataloging-in-Publication data for this book is
available from the Library of Congress.

First Da Capo Press edition 2010
First Da Capo Press paperback edition 2011
HC ISBN 978-0-7382-1353-8
PB ISBN 978-0-7382-1471-9
E-Book ISBN 978-0-7867-4601-9

Published by Da Capo Press
A Member of the Perseus Books Group
www.dacapopress.com

Da Capo Press books are available at special discounts
for bulk purchases in the United States by corporations,
institutions, and other organizations. For more information,
please contact the Special Markets Department at the
Perseus Books Group, 2300 Chestnut Street, Suite 200,
Philadelphia, PA 19103, or call (800) 810-4145, ext. 5000;
or e-mail special.markets@perseusbooks.com.

2 3 4 5 6 7 8 9

CONTENTS

Contents

Contents

INTRODUCTION

So. WHAT DO *I* know now about success?

If you're bold enough to ask so many fabulous, smart, and indisputably *successful* women what *they* know about success, you should have something brilliant to show for it—right? Well, I do. Here are five rules of success I've drawn from working with these ladies on their letters to their younger selves:

Be selfish.

Be bad.

Be dyslexic.

Study your gut.

Don't be men in pink.

Let me explain. I don't mean to suggest that the entrepreneurs, corporate leaders, and accomplished contributors to *What I Know Now about Success* are bad or selfish. Nor would I say that their letters to their younger selves advise selfishness or dyslexia—or caution against pink.

No, these are rules I take responsibility for. They're the shorthand version of all that I learned about these ladies' definitions of success, what stood in their way, and how they overcame roadblocks. They spring from the willingness of these women to pull back the curtain on a critical piece of their interior journeys toward achievement. Frankly, I believe these rules are many times more useful to women—and they *are* for women only—than the standard-issue success advice: *Set clear goals. Persevere. Find a mentor.*

Why? Because success for women is very different than success for men. That's not to say men's and women's journeys, achievements, and feelings about their triumphs never overlap. They do. But the sticking points are different.

There's a resistance to admitting this disparity—as if we fail by being unlike men. As if it's a secret that we are. I've worked with dozens of women who are partners, directors, vice presidents, CFOs, and CEOs of organizations like Goldman Sachs, the Federal Reserve Bank of New York, Microsoft, Genentech, and Johnson & Johnson. Conducting "Letters to My Younger Self" seminars with this rarefied group was a revelation. Here were some of the most powerful women in the business world, and their greatest struggles revolved around learning to ask for what they wanted, not taking failure personally, and that ultimate guilt-inducer, shortchanging their kids and husbands. I know they're out there, but I have yet to talk to a male top executive who agonizes daily about whether his son and daughter would be better off if he were at home with them. I'm not sure I'll ever meet one who has trouble asking for a promotion or a raise. Men have different hurdles.

Before I explain my five success rules for women, I want to acknowledge that I'm ignoring other important, but obvious, dictates. I feel pretty sure you already know that success takes hard work and that it's crucial that you pursue work you love. Also, I won't pretend that one's definition of success never alters. Over the course of the last year, in fact, my personal definition changed from "engaging all of my interests and talents" to "having healthy, directed children" to "knowing what gives meaning to my life." We change. Our circumstances shift. So our perspective on what truly constitutes success adapts.

The five rules may not help you meet every single one of these constantly morphing objectives. But I believe they will aid most women with the whoppers—your biggest efforts and your most significant goals.

Be Selfish That's right. Possibly for the first time in your life, someone is ordering you to be selfish. And here's the irony: my guess is you don't know how. Are you responsible for everyone else's happiness? That is, do you feel accountable for making your kids, your husband, your parents, your boss, and your colleagues happy before pleasing yourself? Some women are so out of practice acting on their own deep desires that they can't actually identify how to end this sentence: "I want…" Years of deferral, self-denial, and manic scurrying to keep all the plates spinning have put a big empty ache at the center of their lives.

Other women are like Mary Lou Quinlan, CEO of Just Ask a Woman (page 103), whose obsession with pleasing everyone else at a Manhattan ad agency prevented her from feeling any joy when she was offered the presidency at a competing firm. As she writes in her letter to her younger self: "This is the biggest promotion of your life. Yet all you can think is: *How could I let everyone down? They'll be so hurt. Who will take care of them if I'm not there? Why did I have to be so selfish as to want this?*"

Obviously I'm not advocating across-the-board egotism. The rule is to be selfish enough to give your wishes an important place at the table and treat them with grave respect. It may sound silly, but it takes practice. Those little inklings of what you could do and what you could become have to be conscientiously petted and coddled and grown. Understanding this now, at sixty-six, Cathie Black, president of Hearst Magazines (page 7), thought the most important question she could pose to her younger self was: "How wide a frame can you put around your future?"

A diagnosis of multiple sclerosis at age forty-two forced Emily Mann, artistic director at McCarter Theatre in Princeton (page 73), to treat herself in a dramatically different way. She wrote: "As a mother, a wife, a director, and an artistic director, you're always taking care of someone else. But now, putting yourself last is no longer an option. You *must* do a better job of safeguarding yourself."

Be Bad This one makes me laugh. Isn't there something delicious about being invited to be *baaad?* Attention all members of the Good Girl Club: This imperative is for you. You know who you are. You follow the rules. You put your head down, do your work, and wait to be noticed for it. If you aren't noticed, you just work harder. You couldn't conceive of taking a new job before you know how to do it perfectly.

When I say "be bad," I mean be daring. Don't wait for permission to act. Be a little devilish. It starts with recognizing which rules have the most power over you—usually the invisible cultural and corporate norms. It took Paula Deen, the cookbook author and Food Network star (page 37), more than twenty years to understand that her crippling fear of public spaces stemmed from her desire to be taken care of.

"I'm a product of the '50s and '60s, where education was not all that important for women," she told me. "I went from Daddy's house to my husband's house. I thought it was completely all right to be taken care of by your man. I mentally and physically fought taking responsibility for myself." For Paula, following society's rules led to helplessness and an anxiety disorder.

Ouidad, founder of a curly-hair empire (page 97), had to be very "bad" to create the life she wanted. Her Lebanese immigrant parents were doubly shamed by her—first because their unmarried daughter lived outside of their home, and second because she was a hairdresser rather than a lawyer, doctor, or accountant. "I was considered crazy, just nuts. My parents and my siblings finally thought there was just no rationalizing with me," she explains.

Being bad also means trashing the strange calculus so many of us carry around, the equation that insists we're allowed only a limited allotment of happiness and success. For example, if you're a big achiever at work, your children can't possibly be well-adjusted, happy people. Or if you engage in work that fulfills you, you can't possibly enjoy financial success. Be naughty enough to flout the guilt, to invent a new arithmetic regarding your share of excellence.

Be Dyslexic A sugarcoated interpretation of this rule is that flaws come bearing gifts—that your weaknesses are counterbalanced by your strengths. But that's a bit of a dodge. In fact, there are three women in this book who struggled with learning disadvantages, and each would tell you that living with this shortcoming seemed to have no redeeming offset for a long time. Barbara Corcoran, who founded a real-estate brokerage worth $70 million (page 25), believed she was stupid in elementary school and beyond. Bobbi Brown, the makeup artist and founder of Bobbi Brown Cosmetics (page 15), almost dropped out of college. Ambassador Nancy Brinker, who founded Susan

G. Komen for the Cure (page 11), was bitterly heartbroken that she could not gain entry to law school.

They wrestled with a more conspicuous imperfection than most of us, so their discoveries on that front are particularly illuminating. They illustrate that the best way to "be dyslexic" is to focus on your strengths rather than try to remedy your weak points. As Barbara says to herself in third grade: "Your people smarts will prove ten times more valuable than all the book smarts you can't get."

Just as they learned to shrug their shoulders over their lacks, these three—and many others in the book—became skilled at detaching emotionally from failures. "If you run into a cement wall, turn right. Or left," advises Nancy. The next time you fail, instead of agonizing and berating yourself for all that you did wrong, think of simply saying: "That didn't work. What's next?" Refuse to take it personally.

Study Your Gut How many times have you heard—or said yourself—"trust your instincts?" And yet few of us perfect this skill—recognizing how our gut speaks and attending to what it's saying. Then, when we do notice that inner voice, we're often comfortable ignoring it because it's singing such an unwelcome song. Governor Christie Whitman's (page 177) instincts told her not to take the job that President Bush offered in the fall of 2000. But really, how many people could turn down a president? She didn't. Yet her gut was right and the job was a disappointment.

Linda Kaplan Thaler, founder of The Kaplan Thaler Group and creator of the "I Don't Wanna Grow Up, I'm a Toys'R'Us Kid" jingle (page 155), received one of the most important messages of her life from her gut during hypnotherapy sessions. Since then, she trusts it. "Your gut has an IQ of 100,000," she tells her younger self.

Don't Be Men in Pink Back in the 1980s, when women began entering the business world in droves, the popular fashion for an aspiring female executive was a business suit and a collared dress shirt topped off with a floppy silk bow tie. Those of us who donned this uninspired uniform now laugh about the way women aped men's business fashions. Our work fashions may be different today, but the truth is that male culture still rules at most American companies for the simple reason that men shaped them and men, in the vast majority of cases, still run them. So it's remarkably easy for women to absorb the prevailing—read: *male*—definitions of successful behavior and leadership in their work.

And there's nothing wrong with that—if they fit you. But for many women, trying to succeed with a bunch of guidelines designed for men prevents them from finding a powerful personal style and sense of meaning at work. Does crushing your competitors under the heel of your boot excite you? Or winning by creating something completely new to your market? Or winning because your role fulfills a larger purpose in your life than to simply earn money?

Everyone's motivation is different. But in my talks with the gifted women in this book and top managers across the country, I found they often had to buck the customary testosterone-tinged corporate culture in order to lay claim to their own authentic leadership. "Don't be men in pink" means resist being recruited by motivations and goals that don't truly speak to your heart.

Mel Robbins, host of *The Mel Robbins Show*, a syndicated radio show (page 109), was so consumed by piling up achievements that would impress others that in law school she began having panic attacks. In her letter, she concludes, "I'm here to tell you there is something great waiting for you in the future. Something that fits you to a T. But you can't find it by desperately excelling at things you don't care about or focusing on proving to other people that you are great."

Personal-finance guru Suze Orman (page 91) frames it this way: "You cannot come into your power until you live a life that is 100 percent authentic." Fashion icon Diane von Furstenberg (page 161) says: "Success is being coherent with who you are." Of course, accomplishing comprehensive authenticity is the job of a lifetime—in or out of the corporate world. It's one I'm certainly still working on. My hope is that this book will inspire you to consider what *you* know now, and share it with other women.

Ellyn Spragins
info@letterstomyyoungerself.com

Sharon Allen
Chairman of Deloitte

You can expand your network and visibility
within the firm no matter where you are.

————

Sharon Allen is a novelty in the business world in more ways than one. As chairman of the board at Deloitte LLP, an accounting and consulting behemoth with nearly $11 billion in annual revenues, she's the highest ranking woman in professional services. Women make up over half of America's labor force, but only 14 percent of the directors of *Fortune* 500 companies are women. That pitiful percentage drops even more if you look at the number of women who run corporate boards.

Not surprisingly, her position has earned her a slew of awards, including being named to *Forbes*'s list of the 100 most powerful women in the world and *Directorship* magazine's list of the 100 most influential people in corporate governance. Because she uses her position not only to evolve and advance Deloitte, but also to generate change for women at work everywhere, to strengthen communities, and to improve higher education, Sharon has also taken on pivotal roles at the Women's Leadership Board at the John F. Kennedy School of Government at Harvard University, the national board of the YMCA, and the Autry National Center.

She maintains that a fuller life is a more honorable life. "I believe in work and life, and that keeping a balance between the two actually creates better opportunity for good ethical behavior. Because when you are not focused only on work, you have a responsibility to a community outside of your corporate relationships," she explains. This is the sort of thinking that led Deloitte to commit to setting a standard of excellence for its profession under Sharon's watch. In 2010, her last year as chairman, Sharon is turning her attention to who her successor will be and the transition ahead.

When we spoke at her midtown-Manhattan office on a sunny fall day, Sharon revealed other ways in which she stands out. She grew up on a farm in Kimberly, Idaho, the youngest of four daughters. Her father was a Stanford-educated potato, bean, and wheat farmer who died when she was only twenty-five. She graduated from the University of Idaho, rather than an Ivy League college. And she spent the first twenty-four years of her career in Boise, Idaho, rather than crisscrossing the globe in pursuit of promotions.

Now fifty-eight, Sharon writes to herself just after she moved to Portland, Oregon in 1997, after twenty-four years in Boise. Two years later she would relocate again—

this time to Los Angeles to run a region larger than her hometown.

Dear Sharon,

Only a couple of weeks ago you and your husband, Richard, attended a Chamber of Commerce event in Boise with 500 people. It couldn't have been more comfortable. You both knew everyone, and you, as the outgoing Chamber chairman and honoree, were the center of attention.

This week you attended a similar gathering of 500 for Portland's Chamber. You didn't know a soul—not even who you *should* know. This isn't the end of the world, of course. But it's a fitting metaphor for the contrast between the comfortable world of friendships, support, and connections that you left and the unexpected challenges that will come with this relocation.

First, the good news. Staying in Boise all those years has given you everything you need for this job and the next. No, you haven't lived in multiple countries and cities. But you've had the good fortune to work in a small office serving large clients. You've recruited talent, brought in new business, watched the receivables—basically run the business in a fuller sense than you would have if you'd been in a large office with more support. There will be more zeroes attached to these familiar functions—but you'll quickly get comfortable because of the breadth of your experience.

The lesson from Boise is that you can expand your network and visibility within the firm no matter where you are.

The lesson from Portland will be, surprisingly, on the personal front. For a family without children, this move is probably harder for you because there's no natural connection with the community you now find yourself in. Your husband is the trailing spouse and won't have the work relationships you're forging.

So, you need to adapt. Come up with a strategy for inserting yourself and Richard into an organization or a board. The extra responsibilities will become joint activities and foster new friendships.

Also, recognize that you don't really have to leave your friendships and connections behind. You never lose them. In fact, their importance will grow as your career progresses. Your family and this extended family of friends give you a core grounding outside the firm that will help you immeasurably as you carry more and more responsibility.

Sharon

CATHIE BLACK
President of Hearst Magazines

*How wide a frame can you
put around your future?*

———

CATHIE BLACK is a captain in an industry convulsed by dramatic change: magazine publishing. As president of Hearst Magazines, a unit of Hearst Corporation, she oversees many of the magazines you love: *Cosmopolitan*, *Esquire*, *Good Housekeeping*, *Food Network Magazine*, *Harper's BAZAAR*, *Marie Claire*, *O, The Oprah Magazine*, *Redbook*, and *Town & Country*, among others. So these days she's knee-deep in figuring out how to turn such print powerhouses into "360°" brands, available worldwide as well as online, on e-readers, and in other digital forms.

The concept is pivotal for Cathie, a straightforward sixty-six-year-old blonde with an easy laugh who married for the second time in her thirties and has an eighteen-year-old daughter and a twenty-two-year-old son. She used the term *360° Life* to describe how women could achieve their full potential in her best-selling 2006 book, *Basic Black: The Essential Guide for Getting Ahead at Work (and in Life)*. The book intersperses advice with personal anecdotes from a career that includes stints at several magazines, including *Ms.*, *City Magazine*, and *USA Today*, where she spent eight years making a resounding success out of a new newspaper that was criticized and scorned by its industry peers.

"When I see what *USA Today* has become, it's an incredible feeling of exhilaration. It was launched under the worst of odds. There wasn't a person on two feet that ever thought this extraordinary undertaking would succeed," she told me with pride.

The newspaper's success is testimony to the effectiveness of two fundamental themes in Cathie's career. She's always pursued products and people she felt intensely enthusiastic about—and she'd rather keep moving forward than look back.

But for this project she did offer to look back at herself as a young, ambitious twenty-eight-year-old working for the feminist Gloria Steinem in New York City at brand new *Ms.* magazine, where she was the manager of advertising sales. She was married, living on the Upper East Side of Manhattan in a two-bedroom apartment, and wrestling with the full life she wanted for herself. "I knew I wanted more—MORE in capital letters," says Cathie. "But it wasn't just about my career. It was also about understanding who I was and what I needed in a partner."

Dear Cathie,

You wanted the job and the title when you went to *Ms.* You thought it would broaden you as a manager.

Now you're realizing how much more complex your situation is. *Ms.*, a new and controversial magazine, is making everyone uncomfortable. Many people, especially men, feel threatened. When you and Gloria go on sales calls, the conference rooms are packed with people who've all come to see what kind of freaks and weirdos run this feminist upstart. Ridiculous as it will seem later on, you're having a hard time persuading advertisers that there is a huge, untapped market of women with income, authority, and decision-making power.

That's the obvious part of your job. There's another part, which will take you much further than simply selling ads for *Ms.*, if you let it. Think deeply about what it actually means for *you* to be a feminist. Consider how you might be an inspiration to the women you're encountering at ad agencies and other companies. Most important: Aspire to be a lot more than you've ever previously imagined. Could you become publisher of a magazine—something no woman has ever done? Could you travel in larger circles?

Why not let your ideas about yourself grow big? How wide a frame can you put around your future?

You're going to have to be honest also about the differences between you and your husband. You can stay in the marriage, hope he'll change and be very supportive, proud and encouraging about your successes. Or own up to what you know you want out of life and part amicably. It's inevitable. Life is too short. Sometimes it will be lonely. But finding your own path, not the one someone else has dictated for you, is what's best for you.

Your partner on the undiscovered path,
Cathie

Ambassador Nancy Brinker
Founder of Susan G. Komen for the Cure

If you run into a cement wall, turn right.
Or left.

WHAT DOES a four-inch piece of pink ribbon, crossed at the ends, signify? What about a three-day walk with thousands of other women?

The Susan G. Komen Race for the Cure, of course. Do you know who put that "of course" into place? Susan G. Komen's younger sister, Nancy Brinker. Hard as it is to remember now, back in the late 1970s, the words *breast cancer* were rarely spoken, and information and treatment options were limited. After being diagnosed at thirty-three, Susan suffered through nine operations, three courses of chemotherapy, and radiation over three years. Throughout she consistently implored her sister, whom she affectionately called "Nanny," to help improve the lot of other women suffering from breast cancer.

Both pragmatic and idealistic, Nancy dedicated herself to nothing less than eradicating the disease. Since she founded it in 1982, Susan G. Komen for the Cure has invested nearly $1.5 billion and become the world's largest grass-roots network of breast-cancer survivors and activists. The Race for the Cure is one of the most successful and best-known fundraising and education events in the world.

Nancy served as U.S. ambassador to Hungary in 2001 and then became chief of protocol for the White House under George W. Bush. She has since returned to Komen for the Cure with the goal of applying all that she has learned in those roles to lead the global anti-cancer movement.

Nancy's achievements—and ambitions—would have looked highly improbable when she was a college graduate. Always a leader in her extracurricular activities, she never-theless struggled academically because of an undiagnosed learning disorder. The learning problems broke her heart when she realized she would not be accepted into a law school. "A lot of things I wanted to do, I couldn't do. I memorized the tests but didn't learn. I desperately wanted to go to law school but I knew I couldn't test well on the LSAT—which made it impossible," she told me.

She says she's always been a round peg trying to fit into a square hole. She didn't learn to do math until she was fifty, when her son, who has the same learning disability, was taught at his school. Even today she avoids driving. "My last job was almost impossible for me because I don't read maps. I'm terrible directionally," she explains

Now sixty-three, Nancy writes to herself when she was crying over not being able to attend law school—and her mother was telling her: "If you fall down, get off your duff and do something about it."

Dear Nancy,

If you run into a cement wall, turn right. Or left. There are several ways to get where you want to go. Not being able to go to law school will lead to something else.

These are hard words to accept when you have your heart set on a particular course. But for you, Nancy, this is one of the most valuable lessons of your life. Take it in.

I can tell you right now that your path will be filled with cement walls, but don't let other people's judgment about that determine where you can go. You'll meet highly educated people who are very snobby about their advanced degrees and who'll look at you like they smell something bad. Don't let it bother you. They've never had to succeed unconventionally. So they won't recognize your true worth.

But people who know you do. Listen to what your mother is telling you: *You're fabulous. Just get up, move on, and do something else.*

Always evolve or become irrelevant,
Nancy

BOBBI BROWN
Founder of Bobbi Brown Cosmetics

You know you're not like everyone else.

IF BOBBI BROWN makeup could speak, it would swipe Billy Joel's lyrics and say: "I love you just the way you are." That's because as a young makeup artist Bobbi brought a new thought to cosmetics: you should look like yourself, even with makeup on.

She considered the pink-toned foundations and lipsticks that were on the market in the late 1980s too artificial-looking. So in 1991, at age thirty-four, she teamed up with a chemist and produced ten brown-based lipstick shades that took the beauty world by storm. Now fifty-two, Bobbi says her credo is "Be who you are." She explains, "That came hard for someone like me. I was never a classic beauty, an athlete, or a brainiac. I was not the tallest or the smartest. As I've gotten older, I've been able to evolve into understanding who I am and feeling comfortable in my own skin."

The trajectory of her business triumph was steep. Bergdorf Goodman showcased her lipsticks in 1991 and

Estée Lauder bought Bobbi Brown Cosmetics, by then a full line including yellow-based foundations, only four years later.

Still CEO of her namesake company and still a hands-and-brushes-on makeup artist (she creates runway looks for designers such as Rachel Roy, J. Mendel, Erin Fetherston, Tory Burch, and Cynthia Rowley), Bobbi has written five how-to books about makeup and has appeared on *Today* and *The Oprah Winfrey Show*. When Bobbi was a student, her parents would never have expected her to achieve such markers of success, she says. Here is Bobbi's letter to herself in high school.

Dear Bobbi,

School is a struggle and you get down on yourself because you're not good at math and science. Your father, a lawyer and a words person, is always reading, and you wonder why you don't take after him more. But don't worry. You'll soon discover that you're creative, a visual learner. And guess what. You're going to be really successful.

Right now, in high school, you know you're not like everyone else. It's not that you don't fit in. You have great friends who love you—but they're all tall, blonde, athletic, and, most annoyingly, they get algebra. Don't let it get you down. Not only will you learn to accept your 5'1" brunette self, one day you'll even open an exercise studio, because you, yes YOU, will discover the power of fitness. In fact, everything you're going through now will inspire your philosophy as a professional makeup artist: help women look like themselves, only prettier and more confident. As for your questionable math skills, know this: you'll have your own CFO one day.

Your feeling of uncertainty as you're trying to figure out who you are and what your life's passion is won't go away overnight. You'll almost drop out of college, but you'll end up transferring to a second university. There, you'll still feel lost. One day your mom will tell you to pretend it's your birthday and ask, "If you could do anything you wanted, what you would do?" You'll say, somewhat hopelessly: "I'd go to Marshall Field's and play with makeup at the cosmetics counter." That's when your mom will help you find Emerson College, where you'll design your own major in theatrical makeup.

The rest won't be easy, but you'll evolve as an artist and launch your own business. You'll even marry the man of your dreams and have three beautiful boys. And, yes, your dad will be so proud. Years from now you'll be walking through an airport, taking your son to his first year at college. You'll call Dad, as you usually do before a trip, and it will hit you: *Oh my God, if you'd told me when I was in high school that one day I'd take my oldest son to*

Stanford University, that I'd be successful and have this amazing life, I'd never have believed it.

xo,
Bobbi

JEAN CHATZKY
Author and Financial Editor at *Today*

It's only in looking back that all the pieces,
including the detours, fit together with
wonderful logic.

JEAN CHATZKY has an uncommon ability to speak while wearing a huge, engaging smile on her face—like you're the only one in the world she really wants to see. This is a skill not to be underestimated, particularly on television, where Jean has been the personal-finance expert on NBC's *Today* since 1995, a frequent authority on *The Oprah Winfrey Show*, and a guest on *Larry King Live* and various shows on MSNBC. I've known that dazzling smile since the early 1990s when Jean and I worked at Smart Money together. My favorite thing about it? It's genuine. She's the real deal—every bit as nice as she seems when she's sitting across from Matt Lauer, cheerfully urging you to swear off credit cards.

In her books, Jean has made a specialty out of pinpointing our most worrisome personal-finance habits and coaxing us out of them. She wrote *Pay It Down! Debt Free on $10 a Day* (its principles now power her interactive program, The Debt Diet) in 2004, even before the scope of America's debt addiction was fully understood. Her 2009 book, *The Difference: How Anyone Can Prosper in Even the Toughest Times*, draws on surveys of more than 5,000 people to discover how the 30 percent of them who described themselves as wealthy or financially comfortable got that way.

Her upcoming, *Dollars and Sense*, targets middle-school kids, who are just beginning to establish their spending and saving habits. "The emphasis on the stock market has been out of proportion. This is a book that is broader in scope and focuses on kids' becoming knowledgeable and responsible about money," she explains.

Many women find it difficult to visualize themselves in a bigger job or on a bigger stage. This was never a problem for Jean, a smart kid who went to the University of Pennsylvania and set her sights on journalism. If anything, she says now, she leaned too hard and too single-mindedly toward her future. After a short stint at the department store G. Fox (where she learned to *never* again take a job just for the money), Jean found a job as an editorial assistant at *Working Woman*, where she developed a knack for writing and reporting about business.

Upon leaving *Working Woman*, Jean bumped up against a big roadblock. "A journalist friend had told me that the *only* place you could go to be a business reporter was *Forbes*, so that's what I wanted to do. But *Fortune, Forbes*, and *Business-Week* wouldn't hire me. They looked at *Working Woman* and thought it was fluff," Jean remembers. She floundered, free-lancing, going to cooking school, and eventually going to work on Wall Street at Dean Witter. Now forty-five, Jean writes to herself at twenty-three after she left *Working Woman*.

Dear Jean,

Don't be in such a rush to secure your journalism career. Slow down. Remember your first job, as an editorial assistant? You were so impatient to make your mark, to report and write that you—oops!—forgot to actually do a good job doing your job. Your eyes were trained on what was coming next—not answering your boss's phone.

There's nothing wrong with focus and tenacity. But your single-minded ambition is working against you right now. Now that the magazines you want to work for have closed the door in your face, you feel panicky. What will it mean if you, the girl who spent almost every spare minute at her college newspaper, can't break into serious business journalism? You're afraid that veering off course means you'll never be able to get back on.

Now is the time that you really have to be willing to take a risk and think outside the box. You can figure this out. And if you take a detour or two, it will not hurt your prospects. Look at it this way. As you move from A to B, from B to C, and so on in your career, your progression won't make sense. It won't look like the perfectly sequential résumé you imagined for yourself. But, in truth, the résumés of most successful people don't look like that. It's only in looking back that all the pieces, including the detours, fit together with wonderful logic.

Think of your dad's hopscotch career and the breadth of your mother's working experiences. Detours and side trips will add depth to your abilities—and your career—in unexpected, invaluable ways.

Slow down and know it will all come together.

A serious journalist, after all,
Jean

BARBARA CORCORAN
Real-Estate Entrepreneur and *Shark Tank* Judge

Your people smarts will prove ten times more
valuable than all the book smarts you can't get.

IT'S ENTIRELY characteristic that the first line in Barbara Corcoran's bio on her Web site is "Barbara Corcoran's credentials include straight D's in high school and college and twenty jobs by the time she turned twenty-three." Witty, unpretentious, and an improbable success, Barbara built The Corcoran Group, a Manhattan-based real-estate brokerage started with a $1,000 loan from a boyfriend, into a high-profile market leader that she sold in 2001 for $70 million.

Since then, the sixty-one-year-old, who looks a little like a blonde elf with a big, telegenic smile, has popped up as a real-estate contributor on NBC's *Today* and is a columnist for the *New York Daily News* and *Redbook*. She's also written two books: *If You Don't Have Big Breasts, Put Ribbons on Your Pigtails: And Other Lessons I Learned from My Mom* and *Nextville: Amazing Places to Live the Rest of Your Life.* When

I spoke to Barbara, on vacation at her summer home on Fire Island, New York, she had recently finished shooting eleven episodes of *Shark Tank*, a new reality show on ABC. On the show, Barbara is one of five self-made millionaires—who are the so-called sharks—competing to invest their own money in entrepreneurial ventures they deem worthy. During the first ten episodes, the sharks—including Barbara, who is the only female shark—invested more than $4 million in 20 deals.

Her television debut is the culmination of a long effort to reinvent herself. Taken aback at how lonely she felt after leaving her community of 1,200 employees at The Corcoran Group, she gamely began calling the heads of the networks. Sure enough, every one returned her call ... because they wanted real-estate advice. "But they never returned my call again. They wrote me off as a nice, aging older woman who thought it would be fun to do a little TV work," she said. "It's been a much more difficult struggle than I expected."

Barbara got her bearings, she says, in the fifth episode, when she realized she had to use her strength in assessing entrepreneurs' character and abilities, rather than pretend to know all the sophisticated financial analysis employed by her fellow shark-investors. As usual, her mother, Florence, provided a key piece of encouragement. After Barbara confessed that she lacked confidence on *Shark Tank*, her mother said, "Oh, Barbara, don't be worried. Just picture Mom and Dad floating over your shoulder cheering you on. You know you always do well."

If it sounds unusual for a woman in her sixties to still be getting support from her mother, instead of the other way around, consider how fundamental Florence has been to Barbara's later achievements. Florence had ten children, who slept in the two bedrooms of their Edgewater, New Jersey, home while she and her husband slept on a foldout couch in the living room. Upon returning from the hospital after giving birth, she would display each new baby to the kids at home and announce the infant's gift. Barbara, she predicted, would have a wonderful imagination.

Her mother's unfailing confidence in Barbara formed an armor that insulated her from despair in elementary school, when she discovered a shocking truth about herself. It happened like this. Barbara floated through first and second grade without learning to read—or worrying about it. But then in third grade Barbara heard some of her classmates laughing when she read aloud. She was sent to a special after-school reading class taught by the dreaded Sister Stella Marie. During the very first session, the nun grabbed Barbara by the ear and said: "If you don't start paying attention, you'll always be stupid."

"That's when it hit me that I had something really bad wrong with me," says Barbara. That afternoon she went into the woods and cried. But at home that night she was still a star to her mother. Florence's reaction to Barbara's reading problems: "Barbara Ann, don't even worry about it. With your imagination, you'll learn to fill in the blanks."

Here Barbara, who has a sixteen-year-old son and a four-year-old daughter, writes to herself in third grade.

Dear Barbara Ann,

Don't be afraid. Stand up and shout out loud and clear enough for everyone to hear: "No, I am NOT stupid."

There's a world of difference between being different and being stupid. It's not a sin when you can't follow directions or don't have the answer. Know that there is no shame in reading out loud and that the other kids' laughter is just a sign of their discomfort with fears of their own. They don't realize they are hearing, for the first time, a different kind of beautiful mind.

You know things the smart kids don't. You create sidewalk chalk games the other kids can't even dream of. You often know what the other kids think before they decide to tell you and can feel the mood in a room the moment you walk in.

You know how to get your sisters to do all your chores. You've learned how to bring humor into the middle of your family's chaos. You know how to build complicated worlds of levels and bridges and alcoves and cliffs and islands and beaches in the little stream behind the house.

Trust yourself, Barbara Ann. What you can't write and spell, you will soon learn how to say.

Hang in there, Barbara Ann. Your talent for daydreaming will come in handy later. And your people smarts will prove ten times more valuable than all the book smarts you can't get.

Be patient with yourself and repeat after me: "I am NOT stupid. I am NOT stupid."

Barbara

PAMELA CRAIG
CFO of Accenture

Nothing is really easy if you're motivated and
want to accomplish a lot in life.

———

THERE'S MUCH to tell you about Pamela Craig. But the most telling detail of our meeting? When she came to my house in Pennington, New Jersey, for our talk, the chief financial officer of Accenture, a global management consulting and services company with more than $21 billion in revenues, brought chocolate. Not supermarket chocolate. A box of John & Kira's, her favorite brand.

Yes, she's a CFO who leads Accenture's finance organization and is a member of the executive leadership team—and she has a warm heart. Pamela, a sandy blonde with a thoughtful manner, has been at Accenture for thirty-one years. She entered the training program of a predecessor firm, Arthur Andersen, straight out of Smith College and found herself in a constantly changing but always absorbing environment. "I liked what we do. I loved the variety. I loved the clients and our people. The whole dynamic of

Accenture always really intrigued me. In all that we do, we're always working with people to help solve problems," she says.

That's one reason the familiar quandary of many working mothers—work outside the home or stay with the kids?—was frustrating for Pamela. She's a problem solver, but this predicament simply doesn't have a clear-cut solution. Her mother, a former home-economics teacher, had equipped her daughter with every conceivable homemaking skill: baking, cooking, sewing, knitting. But even after she had kids, Pamela says: "I really didn't see myself staying at home. It was too confining somehow. I knew I wanted to work."

So she continued in her profession, steadily gaining more and more responsibility with clients in the New York metro region. By the time she was thirty-six, she and her husband, Bob, were living in Westfield, New Jersey. Their sons Robbie and Matt were seven and four. Then she was given a promotion—a portfolio of clients in the northeast and a number of partners to manage. "That was a big step up. A lot of the partners were men who were much older than I, and they weren't too happy about it. So there was a lot of challenge," remembers Pam. And the job involved significantly more travel.

Pam, now fifty-three and a key force behind developing and retaining women at Accenture, writes to herself just after she was promoted at thirty-six.

Dear Pam,

Am I doing the wrong thing here? Should I not be working? Should I be staying home with the boys instead?

These are the questions that have always dogged you as a working mom, but the refrain of second-guessing is louder than ever. You love working. This new job is a huge opportunity—a signal that you have a chance to move up in the company. But it requires traveling and being away from Robbie and Matt overnight several times a month.

No matter how hard you try to predict the things that will happen, and orchestrate the things that *should* happen, something falls through the cracks. Missed doctor's appointments. Last-minute changes in the soccer-practice schedule. Then comes the report from Bob about what went wrong—and it feels like it's your fault.

Organizing the kids' lives while you're away is like trying to tie their shoes with mile-long chopsticks strapped to your arms. When Bob says, "We're out of control," you always reply, "Yes, but we'll get back in control." And, inside you know it will happen again.

Pam, take heart. Here's the fundamental reason you keep questioning your course: your kids are the one thing in your very full life that you can't get wrong. If the kids are not all right, the rest of your life could never feel right.

But how do you know if they are? You really do need to trust your instincts. You have good instincts. Keep your radar up to assess if anything is amiss or if they're going off track. Also appreciate that nothing is really easy if you're motivated, as you are, and want to accomplish a lot in life. And right now it truly is harder, because you can't touch base with the boys' lives the way you want to when you're traveling. How can you check your kid-radar when you're 150 or 2,500 miles away?

But don't mistake the extra stress for a sign that you're doing the wrong thing. Trust that your instincts will ring earsplitting alarm bells, rather than produce nagging questions, if the boys are not all right.

I know you'd like to feel confident that you're doing this perfectly. What a relief that would be! But that kind of stamp of approval isn't available for mothers. You really have to feel your way through it, adjusting as you go. It'll take time before you know you're doing this right, but you are. Remember that what's right for them has a lot to do with what's right for you, too.

Before long they will be navigating their own careers and you cannot yet imagine how your knowledge and experience will be there for them throughout their lives.

Where there is a will, there is a way.

Your friend,
Pam

Paula Deen
Cookbook Author and Food Network Star

*You are mentally and physically refusing to
take responsibility for yourself.*

———

If you had met Paula Deen in high school in Albany, Georgia, you wouldn't have been the least bit surprised. Paulann Hiers had the personality you know: gregarious, bubbly, and funny. As captain of the cheerleading squad, she was practically royalty in the South of the 1960s. "Life was just so great. I had so many friends," recalls Paula.

But between the ages of nineteen and forty she was almost unrecognizable as the same person. It started when her father, Earl, died of a massive stroke at age forty in 1966. Paula, who had married her high-school sweetheart and was only nineteen, was devastated. The night of her father's death she insisted upon sleeping with her mother on one side and her husband on the other.

"I was so scared," she remembers. "I was the apple of Daddy's eye. I was his princess. A girl feels like as long as her daddy is alive nothing can touch her."

She spent a lot of time crying and began to have "crazy thoughts," but wouldn't share them with anybody. As a Baptist, Paula had been taught that everything happens for a reason, so her brain immediately began working out God's motive for taking her father. In her grief and confusion, the answer she concocted was that she was going to die soon and God had decided to spare her father the ruinous pain of living through that experience.

This strange reasoning began to take firmer shape in her mind and then, four years after her father's death, her mother died from cancer. By then she was twenty-three and had two babies under the age of three, a sixteen-year-old younger brother to finish raising, and a firm expectation of imminent death. "I woke up every day waiting to die. I would cough and try to get blood to come up. I was scared to death because of what would happen to my two babies," she recalled.

Instead of abating, Paula's irrational fear sprouted a new branch. She began to be terrified not just of dying, but of dying in public. She started to avoid leaving her home. In time, she could not be outside of her house unless accompanied by her husband—even then, she would venture only a block or two away. "It really hurts me to think I put my needs above my children. I was that crippled. I had to take them out of activities because I couldn't take them," Paula says.

She learned that her fear had a name—agoraphobia—two years later. A neighboring couple in whom she had confided called to tell her to watch Phil Donahue's talk show. "If you turn that on, you're fixing to find out what you have," her neighbor said. She watched and wept.

Her agoraphobia got worse before it got better—eight years later. The day that changed her life came in 1987 after she had spent two months in bed, depressed over her recent move to Savannah, where her husband had taken a new job. One day Paula got out of bed and, she says, it was like "I reached over and flipped the light switch on. In that moment I understood the Serenity Prayer and what I was supposed to be asking God for. I accepted my father's death and my mother's and my death to come. I realized that there are some things you have no control over."

From that split second emerged the adventurous, capable Paula Deen you've come to know. But her letter is written to herself eight years prior, when she was thirty-two years old, sitting at the foot of her bed and watching Phil Donahue with tears streaming down her face.

Paulann,

You are capable. You're a survivor. You'd never know it from the way you've been living, but you are a fighter.

When Daddy died, your world turned upside down. It was such a sharp turn from the perfect life you'd known.

Then when Momma went, there didn't seem to be a safe place in the world for you. You took those deaths, wrestled and kneaded and mashed them around inside your head and somehow came out believing that you're gonna die, too.

Now, here's what you don't realize: this is your way of fighting Daddy's and Momma's deaths. This is how you are mentally and physically refusing to take responsibility for yourself.

Because you are a product of the '50s and '60s, you didn't think education was that important for women. You went from Daddy's house to your husband's house. You thought it was completely all right to be taken care of by your man. Never has it dawned on you that you could be a major breadwinner.

So you keep waiting for your husband to take care of you. You wait for him to stop drinking and behave the way you want. You're putting a lot of pressure on him instead of getting off your ass and up on your own two feet.

There is not one thing you can do for your mother and daddy now—except make them proud of the person that they gave birth to and raised. They did not give birth to a loser, and right now you are a loser.

But it's not too late. Think on this until you really understand it:

God grant me the serenity to accept the things I cannot change; courage to change the things I can; and wisdom to know the difference.

It's gonna feel so damn good to be responsible for yourself.

Paula

NANCE DICCIANI

Former President and CEO of Specialty Materials, a Honeywell Unit

The greatest boundaries that we face in our lives
are very often the ones we ourselves create in
our minds. Don't be self-limiting.

———

ACHIEVEMENT HAS been second nature to Nance Dicciani since she was a kid. But her accomplishments are especially notable because she carved out a career in chemical engineering (after earning her PhD) in the early 1970s, when very few women were in the field, and then fused that specialty to business operations and management. After serving as the superintendent of reservoirs for the Philadelphia Water Department for several years, Nance worked at Air Products and Chemicals and Rohm and Haas in a variety of research, engineering, and management positions.

When she was hired in 2001 as president and CEO of Specialty Materials, a $4.9 billion strategic business group of Honeywell, she became one of the foremost women in the business world. Nance enlisted all of her skills to transform the unit. "We had an extremely broken $3 billion business which was just barely profitable. We sold eleven businesses, amounting to $1.8 billion in revenues, bought $1.8 billion worth of new business, and grew a little over $1.8 billion. We ended up with a very, very profitable $5 billion business," she explains.

When we spoke by phone, Nance's no-nonsense perspective on the effect that success has had on others was revealing. Here's a woman who has steadily moved forward, often against prevailing social norms. On the way up, she noticed there were always people eager to poke holes in someone else's achievements. "Maybe they don't want to put the time in, but they more or less choose to build up their own ego by explaining that someone else's success is luck and they could have done it," she observes. "In fact, most success is just plain old hard work."

A golfer and a private pilot, she says she couldn't begin to count the number of people, particularly women, who have asked her if she is afraid when she is flying a plane. Similarly, when she got the job at Honeywell, people asked her if she could handle it. "They're not really asking me," she says. "What they're expressing is their fear of failure. If you let fear of failure take over, you're just not going to achieve."

After retiring from Honeywell in 2008, Nance joined the boards of Rockwood Holdings, Inc., Praxair, Inc., and Halliburton as well as Villanova University's board of trustees. She is also an operating partner for Advent International, a private equity firm, where her astute managerial skills can be used to remake and improve companies in the firm's portfolio.

Though Nance exhibited leadership skills even as a young kid, by the time she got to tenth grade the allure of becoming one of the popular kids rivaled her interest in academics and extracurricular activities. "I started trying to be a cool kid and was beginning to get rebellious," Nance remembers. What happens to a girl at age thirteen or fourteen may not seem that momentous, but Nance, sixty-two, believes that's when young women make some of the most critical decisions about the rest of their lives. Her letter is to herself at that age, during her quest for popularity.

Dear Nance,

You are one of the fortunate ones! You're growing up in a loving, supportive family with strong values. You have the opportunity for a wonderful education. You've dared to take the "road less traveled" on many occasions and succeeded admirably. You've already conquered challenges, completed tough projects, reached and even surpassed many goals in your young life.

These are admirable traits—apply them broadly. Now that you're beginning high school, don't let peer pressure slow you down. Don't let approval by others stand in your way. Don't wait so long to make a change in any aspect of your life that, in your heart and in your intellect, you know you should and must make. Don't worry about not fitting into the group as you progress—it's better to find another group.

You're not making sacrifices and giving something up. You're making choices. There are a lot of uninspired underachievers out there—leave them behind.

When you are young, the years seem to stretch endlessly in front of you. There is plenty of time for everything you dream of doing. This is a time to be bold, to think big thoughts, to dream big dreams.

Achieving all you are capable of will attract naysayers and opposition. Reaching high and being determined to succeed won't necessarily make you popular. Striving for excellence, rising to a challenge and giving your best is a concept that will weary the lazy and the mediocre because it calls for immediate action. It will bore the sophisticated and amuse the skeptics. And, from firsthand experience, I know it will antagonize others. It's not a popular quest—not more than 5 percent of all people even try.

The greatest boundaries that we face in our lives are very often the ones we ourselves create in our minds. The boundaries of our achievement are primarily self-imposed. Don't be self-limiting.

Have the personal courage to explore and expand your horizons; don't stand still while everything around you is changing. Demand excellence in yourself and in others—and the opportunities you will have are unlimited.

Never let anyone else set boundaries on what you can do, on what you can achieve. That is your responsibility.

Do something you enjoy doing, not something someone else thinks you should do. You'll be better at it, you'll learn from it, and you'll have a sense of achievement that comes from making a contribution and having a positive impact on others along the way. But it is not just about what you do, it's about how you do it and about who you are. Be the *best*. Make a difference. Be persistent and determined; remember the laws of nature dictate that there is only one way you can coast—downhill.

Someone once said that the only future you will ever have is the one you create for yourself. You have it within you to create something spectacular. Why not get on with it?

Start now! I'll be waiting...

The future you

YUE-SAI KAN
Chinese American Entrepreneur and TV Personality

Though you are making mistakes, failing is sometimes the way to move forward.

DREARY, COLD RAIN splashed down in Manhattan on the December day that I visited Yue-Sai Kan, at her magnificent townhouse on Sutton Square, a tiny street lined with formidable beauties. It was the tail end of 2008. The teeth of the global economic slowdown had sunk deeply into businesses around the world, including Yue-Sai's. "It's a terrible time. There is a huge shakedown going on in China. No one knows what will happen," she said to me after we were settled in her living room with hot jasmine tea.

To appreciate how well known Yue-Sai is in China, think of Oprah Winfrey and Martha Stewart combined. A Chinese American who grew up in Hong Kong, she in 1986 produced and hosted *One World*, a television show that introduced millions of Chinese to the outside world and made her a household name. She followed her Emmy Award–winning series with other series and documentaries as well as an entrepreneurial venture that was breathtakingly successful: a line of cosmetics.

Astonishing as it seems, she says that in 1996 no one was using any makeup at all in China. Starting with nine lipsticks, Yue-Sai launched Yue-Sai Cosmetics, a brand now recognized by 90 percent of the Chinese population. Yue-Sai has also written six books, most recently *Exquisite Spaces—25 Top Interior Designers of the World.*

The central theme of Yue-Sai's activities has been to enlarge Chinese aesthetic sensibilities by introducing beauty, style, and graciousness into everyday life. She saw a huge opportunity to do this in another arena—home decor and accessories. "Until the last ten or fifteen years, home always meant to the Chinese a place allotted them by the government. It was always a functional place where you fed yourself and slept," she explains. "It was not a place of beauty or inspiration." Now there's a national fever to own one's own home.

Yue-Sai launched House of Yue-Sai to fill this obvious consumer need—and to establish China's first home-decor brand. "In every area we talk about—bath and bedding, tabletop, decorative accessories—there is no brand that exists in China," she reports. Her first store, a beautiful place that Yue-Sai compares to a Ralph Lauren Home store because it offers consumers a complete home environment, opened at the end of December 2007.

Yue-Sai faced problems in this new business even before the store opened, but by August 2008, when the economy began to sputter, she began to think the enterprise might fail. She would wake up in the middle of the night drenched in sweat. "I have never worked so hard on anything in my life, but it was just not working. I decided to close the store," she recalls. By the time we spoke, she had not had a vacation in two years and felt completely depleted.

Yue-Sai writes to herself about two key lessons that might have helped the House of Yue-Sai survive.

Dear Yue-Sai,

Your idea is brilliant. No doubt about it. You are trying to do for the home what you did in cosmetics. You would like to empower the Chinese to turn their homes into personal, beautiful environments.

But you are being too arrogant. I don't mean that you are lazy or entitled. What I mean is that your self-assurance is making problems for you. Everything you've touched in the past has turned to gold, so you are making two big mistakes.

First, you are choosing your partners poorly. You know your weaknesses, and one of them is managing. You hate managing people. But you're not picking a really good partner who can complement your skills. It's like a marriage, and no less important for your success. You will go through three CEOs in eighteen months, each worse than the one before.

Next, Yue-Sai, you are starting this business too big. The concept of branding the home-decor market is smart, and it's so similar to what you did in cosmetics that you're overlooking some important differences. In cosmetics you can make a variety of products in one factory. But in home decoration you will have more than 150 vendors from ten countries making 3,000 products. The operations are simply more complex than anything you've done before. It would be better to start small and grow.

You will come to see House of Yue-Sai's retail operation as a failure. But because you have only used your own money to capitalize it, you will have only hurt yourself. And though you are making mistakes, failing is sometimes the way to move forward. It's progress.

Yue-Sai

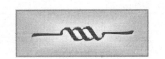

KITTY KOLDING
CEO of House Party

You will be surprised how powerful you can be when you infect others with your enthusiasm.

———

BEAUTIFUL, WITH feathery dark curls and arresting hazel eyes, Kitty Kolding is standing at the spot that's said to define luck: where preparation meets opportunity. As a former entrepreneur of a Chicago company that did research in commercial real estate, she knows what it takes to create value in a start-up company. She's also served as vice president of business development at GetSmart, held a series of high-powered executive jobs at Jupiter Research, and led a private consulting firm as CEO for three years. All of this primed her for her current job: CEO of a brilliant young marketing company called House Party.

Here's the idea. Companies are accustomed to spending millions of dollars to introduce a new skin cream, food product, or TV program to consumers. Just getting noticed, through an ad or a sample, counts as success. House Party's concept is: "We have a way to not only get your product noticed, but to guarantee that it will be used and enjoyed." The company arranges for numerous parties (let's say 1,000) to be thrown on the same day by regular people who invite their friends and family members to come sample products such as Aveeno Positively Ageless potions, Velveeta cheese, or NBC's *Lipstick Jungle*—all past clients of the five-year-old start-up based in Irvington, New York.

"Marketers like this approach because it creates a very direct connection between their product and the consumer in an intimate setting, like her kitchen, with her friends," explains Kitty.

Running a start-up has prompted Kitty to revisit her experience of launching a company at age twenty-four and running it for eight years before selling it to a competitor. While working as a commercial-real-estate appraiser in Chicago in the late 1980s, she found it hard to believe that there was no single source for finding data on sales of comparable properties. She thought to herself: "Well, shoot. I'll just create one." Her naïveté, she says now, was stunning.

Without capital or funding, she started Land Sales Resource (LSR) and began selling the information service to commercial-real-estate brokers, tax lawyers, corporate real-estate departments, and other buyers. With determination and "brute force," she managed to turn it into a pretty successful little business.

Though there were mistakes along the way, the one that still sticks in her craw is the sale of LSR. "I totally, massively, tragically undervalued our business," she says. "I allowed myself to be so dazzled and intimidated by these guys. Once they acquired us for a song, it turned out we were much better than them."

Here Kitty, forty-six, writes to herself at thirty-two about how she might have avoided that mistake and others while running her own company.

Dear Kitty,

What will you take away from the painful and nerve-wracking times you're navigating right now? My wish for you is that you'll more quickly identify the strongest foundations of your character, which are being tested right this minute; that you'll quickly understand how they can define your immediate future and not have to wait ten more years to integrate what you could know now.

If I could change anything for you, it would be to give you the chance to pause and process what you're going through, and to use those insights to gain the confidence you should have. I want you to go through what's ahead with a much stronger sense of your own power and how you can shape your future. There are many lessons to consider, but the ones that will serve you best are these:

- Fear is a poison for which you have an antidote, but you don't know it yet. The antidote is knowing how strong you are, how much you can handle, how you bend but do not break no matter how difficult the things around you become. If you absolutely knew those things, in your core, you would not fear the brutal process you're going through in selling your company. Instead you'd be certain about your ability to battle and win, even if the battle takes longer and is even harder than you might imagine.

- People who have advanced degrees and more re-spected backgrounds than yours are not necessarily smarter than you. Sit down and take an objective in-ventory before you decide you are not as good as somebody else. Be sure to count your greatest assets: your natural leadership abilities and intense drive to succeed. These are potent tools—worth more than a Harvard MBA—not just for you, but for the people around you. You will be surprised how powerful you can be when you infect others with your enthusiasm. Get comfortable with that as quickly as possible so that you never suffer a lack of faith in your ability to learn and adapt while you lead.

- Finding a true partner is one of the most critical things you will do. You *are* better when you have a partner that you can truly trust, rely upon, and function effectively with as a counterbalance to your weaknesses. You're going to make a few bad choices as you learn this, but that is OK. Take the time to process what worked and what didn't. A key: Some relationships shine, grow, and are at their best only within the context of work. You are strong, but once you find a business partner who is truly your equal and who will cover your back, you will experience an entirely different kind of life and work energy that will bring you a joy you haven't felt before.

Kitty

EMILY KWOK
Brazilian Jiu-Jitsu World Champion

This is your life. You must live it for yourself.

———

EMILY KWOK surprised everyone, including herself, when she won the Brazilian Jiu-Jitsu World Championship title in 2007. At the time, she was only a brown belt in this self-defense sport, in which the objective is to land your opponent on the ground and dominate her through grappling (i.e., positioning, submission chokes, and joint locks). She defeated a Brazilian black belt in the Long Beach, California, competition with a score of 17 to 0. She's now a black belt, the first in Canada and one of a small, elite group of about twenty competitive female black belts in the world.

"Before my involvement in jiu-jitsu, I didn't think I was competitive. I remember falling off the monkey bars as a kid and never attempting to get back on them again," she says. But athleticism and competitiveness are incidental gifts that the sport has brought to twenty-nine-year-old Emily. Through jiu-jitsu, Emily has fundamentally altered herself, becoming more centered and confident—characteristics that had been missing ever since her relationship with her father ruptured when she was fourteen. "Jiu-jitsu has been a vehicle for better understanding how I interact with the world."

Born to a Japanese mother and a Chinese father in Aomori, Japan, Emily emigrated with her family to Vancouver, Canada, in the early 1980s. Though the family assimilated to its new environment, at home the atmosphere was culturally very stereotypically Asian, says Emily. There was very little communication and she and her younger sister were expected to choose white-collar professions. Emily felt she never measured up. "I was surrounded by a sense of disapproval. I felt my father never found in me what he was looking for," she explains.

She developed a fierce sense of independence at a young age. She attended and graduated from the Emily Carr Institute, a prestigious Canadian art school, despite her parents' disapproval. At nineteen she embarked on a bicoastal life in which she resided part-time in New York City; this lasted for three years. It wasn't until 2001 that she took up jiu-jitsu, initially as a hobby, during one of her summers in New York. As the sport gradually became her chief focus, Emily settled in New Jersey, marrying Gerry Hurtado, a firefighter, in 2008.

In addition to competing and working as a program director for a large martial-arts academy, Emily is involved in launching a series of women's grappling camps. Because so few women are pursuing jiu-jitsu, she says, the camps fill a need for jiu-jitsu practitioners who rarely have the chance to get to know other women in the sport.

Though she is in close touch with her mother, Emily hasn't spoken directly to her father since he kicked her out of the house when she was fourteen. She was eating dinner at the kitchen table with her mother and sister when her father came home angry. "He threw his keys onto the table and yelled at me, asking, 'Why are the garbage cans still outside?'" remembers Emily. When she didn't know how to answer him, he told her to get the hell out of the house, she says.

She walked for thirty minutes to a friend's house. The friend's mother said she could stay but asked that she call home to tell her parents where she was. As Emily recalls, her father began yelling at her again. Though she went back home, Emily says, "It changed the way I felt about my family. I realized I had to keep doing what I wanted for myself because I would never be able to get his approval."

Her letter is to her younger self just after she was told to leave the house at fourteen.

Dear Emily,

I know you are feeling confused and angry right now. It's difficult to understand the actions of others. Sometimes you are just not meant to. Because you live with someone who is not capable of giving you approval, you take too many things personally.

Soon it will be time to separate what brings you happiness from what brings your parents happiness—or what they imply will make them happy. Continually seeking their approval will condition you to always work harder, take on new challenges, and strive to be the best at everything you do. But eventually, you must see that rather than continue to seek *their* approval, you must learn to trust in your own.

Don't let the fear or insecurities of others dictate the path that you are meant to follow. Do not let their negativity affect who you are discovering yourself to be. Your spirit will be tried many times—by loneliness, jealousy, fear, and ego—but it will not break. Your spirit fought very hard to be of this earth, and it will not be extinguished quietly.

This is your life, Emily. You must live it for yourself. Do not avoid what is unknown because it makes others uncomfortable. Seek the answers you desire to satisfy yourself. Anything is possible and every unexpected achievement is waiting for you to invest your potential in.

Trust in your heart and you will see that life will take care of you.

Your future self,
Emily

Liz Lange

Founder of Liz Lange Maternity

*Your business will be an act of self-expression
that will bring you joy.*

LIZ LANGE's concept was an alien notion in 1996. Maternity clothes in beautiful fabrics? Maternity clothes that are expensive? Maternity clothes that hug a pregnant belly rather than drape it like a pup tent?

Thanks, but no thanks. That's more or less what the merchants at Macy's, Bloomingdale's, Saks, Bergdorf Goodman, and other department stores said to Liz. If you want to do that, she remembers them telling her, be prepared to sell the clothes yourself because we do not want to be in that business—it's a terrible business.

Meanwhile, twenty-nine-year-old Liz, a hard-core fashion and shopping enthusiast, saw her pregnant friends buying expensive designer clothes and then paying to have them altered. She also noticed that they looked better when they squeezed themselves into stretchy, clingy outfits than when they wore big, boxy clothes. "Everything I saw among my pregnant friends led me to believe that the retailers were wrong," she remembers.

They were wrong, of course. Liz Lange Maternity was launched in 1997, and its close-fitting maternity fashions lent pregnancy a whole new modern look. While dressing her friends with her new styles, Liz, who is the niece of financier Saul Steinberg, was also aggressive about getting her designs onto the bellies of pregnant celebrities. Her fresh take on maternity fashion played perfectly to the bump-watch and pregnancy-pride trends in Hollywood and elsewhere.

By 2002 Liz's company had three stores and a clothing line at Target. In 2007 she sold it to Bluestar Alliance for a reported $50 to $60 million, though she remains the public face of the company and consults on designs and other key elements. She is the only maternity designer to have shown at New York Fashion Week and was the first to focus on maternity activewear, with her 2001 deal to produce Liz Lange for Nike.

And yet, sitting in her midtown office, hands periodically snaking through her long, glossy dark hair, Liz calls herself an "accidental entrepreneur." The reason: A comparative-literature major at Brown, she never thought that someone could create a serious career out of a love of fashion and shopping. She laughs as she describes her talent: "I can just walk into a store and immediately zero in on what to try on. It just comes naturally to me."

Liz dithered longer than she needed to in starting the company, she says, because she was listening to all the retail experts who said fashionable, close-fitting maternity wear would never fly. "I wish I had understood that they were all just people—and they could be wrong. Anyone can have a great idea," she says.

Now forty-three and a cervical-cancer survivor, Liz is the mother of an eleven-year-old son and a nine-year-old daughter. She writes to herself when she was thinking about launching her company in 1996.

Dear Liz,

Looking back at you, at twenty-nine, I'm amazed.

I'm so different now—OK, we're so different now. You should go ahead and start your company *now*. Later on you'll hear a lot of stuff about entrepreneurial instincts and risk taking, but, honestly, that's not the important part of why you should do it. For you, growing your company will be a fabulous way of growing yourself as a person.

For example, you know how you always say that you're not very competitive...like it's a negative thing? Guess what. You'll discover you are competitive. Competition is normal and healthy and will spur you to make your business the best it can be.

Remember your disastrous public speaking experience in sixth grade? You resolved that you would never,

ever give a speech again. You decided that was just not you. And yet, Liz, you will give a keynote speech—your first since sixth grade—at the Waldorf Astoria in front of 2,000 people. After that you will give speeches all the time. Believe it.

The point I'm making is not that competition is inherently good or that making speeches matters. The point is that you've walled yourself off from entire spheres of activity for no good reason. Inside you wonder if you could possibly be allowed to have a career based on activities you find fun. Or if you can actually see a viable opportunity that more experienced, older people have missed.

Of course you can! You are being too severe about yourself. People often treat business as though it's terribly complex and serious. Don't buy that. Of course there will be hard work. But your business will be an act of self-expression that will bring you joy and spur you to grow far beyond your self-imposed boundaries.

With excitement about what's ahead for you,
Liz

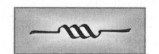

EMILY MANN
Playwright and Artistic Director of McCarter Theatre

Putting yourself last is no longer an option.

"I OFTEN FEEL I would be a much less happy person if I had not had this disease," says Emily Mann. She's referring to multiple sclerosis, not an ingredient that most people would include in their recipe for a happy life. But for Emily, a congenial fifty-eight-year-old with a gift for instant rapport, MS upended and then reordered her life.

On the summer day we met at McCarter Theatre, in Princeton, New Jersey, she emerged from her office having just crafted a delicate reply to an infuriating e-mail. Her long dark hair was pushed into the messy bun style favored by college students. Her brain was still half snagged on the e-mail exchange. She took one look at me, smiled, and then clapped her hands to her face. "Oh! I was going to put on makeup," she exclaimed.

Yeah, she's got other things on her mind. By my count, during the last twenty years Emily has had four full-time careers—simultaneously. As an artistic director, she's overseen more than ninety productions and turned McCarter into a regional theater powerhouse, for which it won a Tony in 1994. As a playwright, she's tackled knotty, controversial topics and written some of the most popular and widely produced plays in the country, including *Having Our Say*, which racked up three Tony nominations (as well as Peabody and Christopher awards for the screenplay) and returned to McCarter in the fall of 2009 to inaugurate Mann's twentieth-anniversary season.

Those are just the first two jobs. She also directs her own and others' plays, including the Pulitzer Prize–winning *Anna in the Tropics*, at McCarter and on Broadway, and *Me, Myself and I*, an Edward Albee work commissioned by Mann, produced at McCarter, and now slated to open on Broadway in August 2010. And finally, she's an ardent teacher and an advocate for unknown playwrights.

"It's not a meritocracy, you know," she says, with a wry shake of her head. "You can't make it in theater without a champion." Compassion—and indignation—on behalf of the underdog, the misrepresented, and folks on the losing end of a raw deal are the themes that pull together Emily's fourfold career. After she learned in 1994 that she has MS, she added one more activity to her calendar: speaking to people newly diagnosed with the disease.

Multiple sclerosis muscled its way into Emily's life while she was traveling to a country home owned by Gary Mailman, her fiancé at the time, in upstate New York. It began as a tingling in her leg. By the next morning the entire right side of her body had gone numb. An emergency-room doctor at a nearby hospital dismissed their concerns, saying: "It's all in her mind."

Emily, who had just learned that McCarter had won the Tony Award for Outstanding Regional Theater, decided to go shopping with a friend to find a dress for the awards ceremony, even though she felt odd. "We were in some fabulous shop downtown when I reached out my hand, fell, and started crying. I thought I had a brain tumor," she remembers. Expecting to die, Emily asked her friend to help Gary take care of her ten-year-old son, Nicholas.

She was taken to New York Hospital and within a day learned she had MS. "I thought my life was over. It was a horrifying time," says Emily. She decided the honorable thing would be to release Gary from their engagement. He said: "Oh no. I am not going anywhere."

She also thought McCarter should not be burdened with an invalid artistic director. But the board said it would provide whatever Emily needed to stay on.

"What saved me was the extraordinary support I got," she says. A healer recommended by Bill Cosby's wife, Camille, helped her manage several aspects of the disease. But by 1999 she was going downhill and arrived at her neurologist's office unable to walk or function. He experimented with a series of new drugs and finally found the right combination of medications. Emily has been in full remission for the last four years.

Still, it's been a harrowing road. Here she writes to herself at forty-two, after the diagnosis.

Dear Emily,

I won't try to soften the blow. I know exactly how terrified you are. Nothing I say will change the hard, ugly fact that your body is now a hostage to MS.

But you are going to be lucky—hard as that is to believe. Soon, you will learn how to think through the pain around your middle and the numbness throughout your body; how to put your concentration on a different level. Actors and athletes do this all the time. They find a way to move past and through physical discomfort. You'll find out how to concentrate on a higher level than you could before you got ill. And your work will be the better for it.

Even more important are the messages this disease carries for you.

For example, when you have MS, you lose your balance and fall down. In order to rebuild your life you'll have to find balance mentally, physically, and emotionally. You will discover yoga and a whole world will open up to you.

So far, imbalance has ruled. You've worked around the clock—exhaustion be damned—to make McCarter a huge success. As a mother, a wife, a director, and an artistic director, you're always taking care of someone else. But now, putting yourself last is no longer an option. You *must* do a better job of safeguarding yourself. First, understand that you can only do so much each day. Decide what's most important and jettison the rest. In so doing, you will find out what really matters in life. And who really matters. Your family life and your work will become stronger and richer with that knowledge.

The second imperative. Learn how to ask for help. It's shocking, but people *want* to help. Your huge life lesson is to discover that when you ask for help you are allowing other people to give. This is a precious exchange. So, how you accept people's care is very important. Do so with deep and profound gratitude. And love.

With a full heart,
Emily

TRISH McEVOY

Makeup Artist and Founder of Trish McEvoy

Enlist reason over emotion; keep your head
down and look for the solution.

———

I MET TRISH in 2005 when I interviewed her for *What I Know Now: Letters to My Younger Self*, my first book. She invited me into her dreamy Manhattan apartment and spent several hours with me. During that time she offered to connect me to her speech coach and photographer, fielded a call from an employee, which ended with her giving Broadway theater tickets to the staffer, and seemed to be fascinated with the small details of my life, even though we were supposed to be talking about hers.

I soon learned that generosity and personal warmth pour out of this tiny, porcelain beauty every day. She is "other focused," with a knack for making your concern her concern. "I love to see the joy a woman feels when she looks at her reflection and feels pretty. Makeup empowers women at the same time as it creates intimacy between them," she told me. Trish's skill at building relationships is especially clear at her company, where she calls her employees a second family.

After falling in love with and marrying Ronald Sherman, a dermatologist, Trish pioneered the marriage of beauty and science that is now commonplace by opening in 1978 the first medi-spa, the Dr. Ronald Sherman/Trish McEvoy Skin Care Center in New York. In addition to her fabulously functional makeup, clean scents, and candles, you may also be familiar with the famous Trish McEvoy "planner," a notebook-style cosmetic holder with Lucite "pages" in it.

In thinking about what she knows now about success, Trish believes one of her most important business experiences occurred during the economic meltdown that began in the second half of 2008. By August she began to face the reality of job cuts. "It was very personal. These are my people," she explains. Here she writes to herself about the distressing challenges and unexpected upside of moving through that brutal time period.

Dear Trish,

Success. You've always defined success by *how* you live your life and *who* is in your life. The quality of each day is how you measure happiness, and nothing exhilarates you like the development of people, the growing of a business, seeing your friends and family happy. But on the

path to success, business, just like life, throws you curve-
balls—and boy are you getting a curveball in 2008.

Nothing has ever prepared you for the economic
storm that you're facing. On a personal level, your
mother's Alzheimer's is getting worse, as is your honey's
arthritis of the neck. You suddenly lose a dear friend and
family member. And all this against the backdrop of an international economic downturn. For the first time you're
going to have to eliminate jobs and cut salaries of employees. That hurts. These aren't faceless names—these
are people you know. You're part of their lives. The
painful prospects and the uncertainty are keeping you
awake at night.

Take a deep breath, Trish. Do what you've always done.
Take it one step at a time. Get experts to help you. For
your mother it will be the perfect caretaker, Bunny. For
your husband it will be the perfect trainer, Monica. For
your business it will be taking a step back. You and your
senior management team will have to take a close look at
how to rapidly storm-proof your business for the turbulent
year ahead. Here is what you need to do: enlist reason
over emotion; keep your head down and look for the solution. And this is key: *there is always a solution.*

You have been blessed to enjoy decades of steady
growth—2007 was a banner year—and now you are having
to draw upon all the experience of your years to grow

your business in spite of the economic climate. You have to perform triage, and critical decisions must be made, quickly. Your level-headed husband and seasoned vice presidents, Joanne Pigozzi and Geri Emmett, who are also your best friends, will help you make the necessary changes to take your business to the next level even as the media horrible-izes and retail seizes up.

Lucky for you, your life's work is your passion. Watching a woman walk away with her face looking the way she always wanted it to look and the knowledge to make it look that way herself is a joy that never fades. And you are so blessed to be in a self-love industry that is a source of joy, entertainment, confidence, and personal care to women. In fact, you may be needed now more than ever. The challenge: there will be less room at the top, so you need to pull out all the stops to be the best you have ever been.

The silver lining at any challenging time is that it is then that you learn. Right now you are being given the opportunity to get even better at what you do in order to weather this storm. When you come out on the other side—*and you will come out on the other side*—you and your team will be stronger, wiser, more adaptable to change, and more close-knit than ever before. You will learn that *there is always opportunity*. Ironically, you will grow in more new ways than you would have if the bubble had never burst because *this is your time*.

Your focus has always been to make it easy for women to enhance their beauty, and the very products and philosophies that have always set you apart will be what pull you through now. Now, more than ever, women need multifunctionality; the perfect shades that flatter and can be counted on; and systems that organize, save space, and eliminate stress and waste. In short, we need to put on our game faces quickly and easily.

And people. You are only as good as the people on your team, and your team will take your breath away. Cream will always rise to the top, and you have a winning team whose objective is to win whether times are good or bad. Happily, your passion for relationships with staying power will be your saving grace on both the client and the team-member sides. Having grown your company one relationship at a time, you will realize that the best investment you've ever made has been in people.

You will keep growing, Trish, but you will never outgrow the core principles that will get you through this year and define who you are. No matter what is going on around you, look inside, and never stray too far from what you believe.

You're gonna be more than all right.

Love,
Trish

SOLEDAD O'BRIEN
CNN Anchor and Special Correspondent

There is opportunity—and sometimes joy—
in chaos and the unknown.

"DEFINITELY A Type A personality."

"Every minute on my Blackberry is accounted for."

"I'm the kind of person who always chooses the same familiar route for my daily run in any given city, rather than explore a new course."

This, in part, was how Soledad O'Brien described herself when we spoke on the phone. "I like to know exactly what's ahead," she explains.

That's impossible, of course, as someone in the news business understands all too well. But wringing efficiency out of every moment is a critical job skill when you're a CNN anchor, a special correspondent for CNN's *Special Investigations Unit*, and the mother of four kids under the age of ten. Soledad also covers political news as part of CNN's "best political team on television," and in 2009 completed *CNN Presents: Black in America,* six hours of stereotype-busting documentary and reports.

Bringing complexity and fresh nuance to stale topics is a talent that stems from Soledad's background. Her full name is María de la Soledad Teresa O'Brien. She is the fifth child of six born to an Afro-Cuban mother and an Australian-Irish father, both of whom were educators and immigrants. All six children went to Harvard. Soledad had mapped out a career in medicine, as had a brother and sister, from an early age. It was a shock when she realized during her senior year in college that she wanted to go into journalism rather than be a doctor.

"I might as well have sprouted another head," she says, remembering how alien this new career choice seemed to her and her family. "I had no idea how to become a writer. It was unknown territory."

She figured it out, eventually covering some of the globe's most urgent stories, such as Hurricane Katrina and the tsunami in Phuket, Thailand, and winning awards, such as the 2007 Gracie Allen Award and, in 2008, the first annual Soledad O'Brien Freedom's Voice Award, which was created by Community Voices at the Morehouse School of Medicine to honor catalysts for social change.

Now forty-four, Soledad chose to write to herself in her mid-twenties, which was a key period in her career. At then-NBC affiliate WBZ-TV in Boston, she had been an associate producer and news writer. Then, in 1989, she moved to NBC affiliate KRON in San Francisco, where she had to master a new skill as a local reporter.

Dear Soledad,

There is opportunity—and sometimes joy—in chaos and the unknown. I suspect you'll find this extremely hard to believe. For someone like you, who is most deeply secure when your path and every step on it are completely mapped out, "the unknown" sounds like being lost. And not just lost in the sense of having momentarily veered off course. Lost, as in completely adrift, not findable. Without understanding why, you've always felt that if you take one or two steps off the golden, preordained path you might never be able to get back on.

Being highly organized with concrete goals has helped you be productive, without a doubt. But Soledad—open up the door to a little more uncertainty! Honestly, it's not a weakness to live this way. Moving forward *without* knowing where it will lead will be excellent for your career and your personal life.

It's liberating. If you stop obsessing about getting your ticket punched at all the "right" stations, you'll be able to take opportunities that you wouldn't otherwise consider. Don't worry about losing control. Accepting ambiguity will free you to think about what's right for you.

At the start of your career you're worried you're not a great reporter. You have two choices about that. You can agonize over the proven, correct process for becoming better and try to hurry it up. You can constantly compare yourself unfavorably to other reporters. Or... you can accept that there is no single right path and let yourself grow at the best possible pace *for you.*

In TV news it's very easy to compete with everyone else. What you have to do, though, is compete with yourself. Rather than just sprint to a title, focus on the integrity of doing work you like. Value the projects you get to be a part of. Those things are far more important than racing against the clock, trying to beat the people around you.

To remind you, here's something J.R.R. Tolkien wrote: "Not all those who wander are lost."

Your slightly more chaotic future self,
Soledad

Suze Orman
Personal-Finance Author, Columnist, and PBS Star

You cannot come into your power until you live
a life that is 100 percent authentic.

Some public figures seem to spring onto our radar fully formed and ubiquitous. Suze Orman, with her bronzed face, golden hair, and 1,000 watt smile, is one of them. She's a contributing editor to *O, The Oprah Magazine* and has her own Saturday-night show on CNBC, not to mention a string of best-selling books and personal-finance products. She's written, co-produced, and hosted six PBS specials and is the most successful fundraiser in the history of public television. So, would it surprise you to know that she didn't write her first book (*You've Earned It, Don't Lose It*) until she was forty-four? And that the book that really put her on the map—*The Nine Steps to Financial Freedom*, with 3.1 million copies in print—didn't come out until she was forty-six?

Suze became ultrasuccessful relatively late. And despite appearances to the contrary, even when it arrived, that success had some giant holes in it. "I always had a feeling that everybody else was better than me," she told me when we spoke by phone. "Everybody else was smarter. Everybody else had better parents, had more money, had more everything than I did."

As a kid, she says, she stole money from her dad's pockets to buy gifts for her friends. "I really, really thought the only reason people would ever like me was if I gave them something," she recalls. When her high-school algebra teacher let her grade tests, she changed the scores on her friends' tests to help secure their good opinion of her.

The odd thing about Suze's profound sense of inadequacy is that it did not lessen as she gradually achieved more and more. You may be familiar with some of her story. She had a speech impediment that hurt her reading ability and cemented her idea of herself as "dumb." Yet she attended and graduated from college. She was a waitress at the Buttercup Bakery in Berkeley, California, earning $400 per month, for seven years. But a group of her customers were so confident in Suze—a "counter girl with porcelain blue eyes and a million-dollar personality," as one described her—that they loaned her $50,000 to open her own restaurant. She became a stockbroker at Merrill Lynch instead, after her broker there lost the stake of loaned money.

By the time she was forty-seven she had two books under her belt, financial success, and the first sketchy notion that just maybe she, the girl with the speech impediment who still said "shunt" for "shouldn't" and "dint" for "didn't," might have something worthwhile of her own to say. "I still asked everybody else what they thought about everything because I thought everyone else would know more than I did," she recalls. "But I was starting to know my own thoughts because when I went on book tour by myself, I had to do things all alone and with people who didn't know me. I was able to be anybody I wanted to be." It was the beginning of Suze having enough confidence to show her true self to the world.

Suze, now fifty-eight, lives and travels with her partner, Kathy Travis, known as KT, a successful businesswoman who is now Suze's business manager. In her letter Suze is writing to herself at age forty-eight, two years before she met KT, during a month in which she flew 70,000 miles to twenty-one different cities.

Dear Suze,

You're crisscrossing the country. Boston. Seattle. New York. California. Back and forth, using your time inefficiently because all the PBS stations are deciding they want your *Nine Steps* special at the last moment. But you're delighted to be working 24/7. Why? Truthfully, anything would be better than having to be home with your partner. You hate the relationship you're in, which is now in its sixth year.

You know this to be true. You're waiting, praying, and hoping that this woman will find someone else and go on her merry way. You know very well that if you make a change, this person will want to come after you with a lawsuit.

Suze, you don't flinch from this knowledge—and yet you continue to live this way. Staying in a horrific relationship shows what you believe to be true about yourself.

You believe that you don't deserve the best in every part of your life. You think you need to settle when it comes to personal relations. You are not as good as or better than others, Suze Orman. You can't do certain things because it would hurt someone else's feelings.

You are living a lie.

Suze, you do not have a choice. You have to stop. It does not matter if you lose every penny. You will make it again. It's not about the money—it's about living the truth. You will not—you cannot—come into your power until you live a life that is 100 percent authentic every moment of the day, in every way.

It will be hard. You won't have the courage to enter your next phase of life as an authentic woman until you meet the right woman. But when you finally do, you will recognize pure goodness and uncover a new cache of integrity and energy contained inside you. You will understand that your job is not just to be the greatest personal financial advisor in the U.S.—it's to make people feel like they are great, which they are.

You already know that if you honor people first, the money will come. But what you will understand in a new way is that if you honor the person *you* are first, you'll achieve the greatest attainment of all: looking in the mirror into your eyes and liking the eyes that look back at you.

A perfect relationship is waiting for you,
Suze

Ouidad

Curly-Hair Entrepreneur and
Founder of Ouidad

Stay focused. You're not doing a bad thing.

————

IF YOU THINK it sounds strange to say that someone is saving the world from curly-hair angst, that's probably because you have straight hair. As the sister of a woman whose curly hair was tortured into submission with knit ski hats, head wraps made from support panty hose, and Dippity Do for a good chunk of her life, I knew Ouidad was on a mission of empowerment when I met her twenty-four years ago.

Born in Lebanon, Ouidad and her American-born husband, Peter Wise, have grown Ouidad, their company, from a single Manhattan salon into a curly-hair empire with fifty-two Ouidad-certified salons, twenty-two products, and between $10 million and $20 million in revenues. In 2007 the potential for further growth attracted investor JH Partners, a San Francisco private-equity firm whose portfolio of companies has included Bare Escentuals, NapaStyle, Design

Within Reach, and Frette. Sephora began stocking stores with Ouidad products in 2009.

All of this is built on the horrible relationship that many curly-headed women have with their hair. Often enslaved to chemicals, straightening, and blow-outs, curly girls have an epiphany when they encounter Ouidad; her special cutting technique, "carving and slicing"; and her products. "It's been absolutely wonderful to be able to change their lives— to bring them out of hiding from the rain, to release them from avoiding swimming and to free them from hours of straightening," says Ouidad, whose shoulder-length dark curls frame a beautiful, often mischievous smile.

In many ways, her spunk makes her success seem inevitable. As a girl, Ouidad loved to carry her father's briefcase and used to hide in his car so that she could go to work with him. Though he had two sons and two daughters, she says, her personality always made him feel he had three sons and one daughter. "I was always aggressive. I was clever and smart at school. I used to drive my mother crazy because I wore shorts under my skirts," she remembers.

But in truth, Ouidad's achievement faced long odds because of the cultural traditions she was steeped in. Lebanese culture was sophisticated and urbane, but at the same time Middle Eastern and male-dominated. Being a single girl living outside her parents' home, as she was after she moved from her family home in Rhode Island to New

York in 1978, was cause for shame. That she was a hairdresser, rather than a professional, doubled the disgrace for her parents.

Ever strong-willed, Ouidad could see clearly what she wanted—her own career and, ultimately, her own salon in Manhattan—and she understood that she would need to fight her mother to accomplish it. "I knew I had to challenge her so I could break away from home and break away from the culture," she remembers. The excruciating element to this choice was that her mother was ill with breast cancer, though the diagnosis wasn't immediately clear when she fell sick in 1977.

Ouidad went to New York when she was twenty, initially to style hair for a Broadway show. But then she was forced into freelancing. Her father and mother cut her off financially, hoping that she would crash and come home with her tail between her legs. Instead, she figured out how to support herself and continued to visit home regularly. When her mother was in the hospital for two years, Ouidad routinely worked in New York for three or four days, boarded a late train, and arrived at Massachusetts General Hospital in the morning. "Every time I was home in Rhode Island she would talk to me about moving back. I questioned myself every day," she recalls.

On one occasion her mother was so distraught when Ouidad was at the door, about to leave, that she said: "I hope you get hit by a Mack truck and get killed." At that moment, her mother's shame outweighed all of her other emotions, explains Ouidad.

Here fifty-two-year-old Ouidad writes to herself at twenty-one.

Dear Ouidad,

You know you're going to lose her. Every day you know that if you weren't chasing your dream in New York you could be there.

You also feel the urgency of staying on your course. You can see so clearly what is right for you. You sense your father's support. His voice is always in the back of your head, saying, *You can accomplish anything you want.*

Remember this: you haven't deserted Mama. Despite her frustration and her anger, you travel to be with her every week. And when you are with her, you are there 100 percent. You'll never feel guilty because you know how fully you're there with her.

Stay focused. You're not doing a bad thing. It helps that you can compartmentalize, giving everything to your New York life when you are in New York and all of your attention to your mother and family when you are home. This ability will always protect you.

Life goes on. Remember how when you were little you used to tell your father that you wanted to run your own country? You will create a company that feels like its own world, complete with citizens you help and protect. Your father will tell you when you finally open your salon: "You know, I'm really proud of you."

Your mother, though she will be gone by then, would say the same. The gift you are giving her by sticking to your plan is that she'll know, before the end, that she doesn't have to worry about you.

Feeling wonderful about our relationship with Mama and completely content,
Ouidad

MARY LOU QUINLAN
Author and CEO of Just Ask a Woman

You are not in charge of everyone else's happiness.

———

NICKNAMED SMILEY and Bright Eyes as a girl, Mary Lou Quinlan could have been president of the Type A Good Girl Club. She had a perfect attendance record, earned straight As, and won award after award in school—all the while acting relentlessly cheerful. She not only wanted to be the best, she wanted to make everyone happy along the way. Her zeal for success and pleasing others translated into never saying no at work and a string of promotions at Avon and Manhattan advertising agencies.

But Mary Lou's big heart and work-first-last-and-always commitment led to a distorted sensibility in her relationships. She came late, or didn't show at all, to friends' events. She deferred get-togethers with her family. Meanwhile, she connected intensively with work friends. "Too often, my employees, colleagues, clients, and bosses got the best of my love. Their phone calls were returned immediately. I never missed their meetings. I celebrated their birthdays with presents and parties," she wrote in *Time Off for Good Behavior.*

Her tenacious embrace of work and success won her the CEO position at NW Ayer. But the relentless schedule also drove her—ridiculous as it sounds—to fantasize about having a small accident as a way to get time off. Finally, she took a five-week break, decided to quit the corporate rat race, and, in 1999, started her own company, Just Ask a Woman. A market-research consulting firm, the business is built around a list that Mary Lou entitled "What I love to do and am really good at."

Just Ask a Woman tossed out the tired, *Mad Men* mode of research, in which consumers are observed from behind a one-way window. Instead Mary Lou and her staff invite a group of women to sit together on a stage with a microphone in a talk-show format with a live audience in front of them. Discussion in this arrangement "creates a different dynamic. No one else is in control. The women feel freer and stronger and can have a more open exchange of opinions," explains Mary Lou.

It's not just the format that creates a special dynamic, of course. Mary Lou still beams high-wattage empathy and warmth to everyone around her. The difference is that now the demands on her charm aren't growing exponentially. "I had no desire to have a lot of employees and the worries that go with that," she says with a big smile, smoothing back her auburn hair. "I couldn't have put the Big Job further behind me if I tried."

Just Ask a Woman has canvassed approximately 15,000 women about everything from fibromyalgia to child rearing. Mary Lou gives speeches and writes books (*Just Ask a Woman: Cracking the Code of What Women Want and How They Buy*; *Time Off for Good Behavior: How Hardworking Women Can Take a Break and Change Their Lives*; and *What She's Not Telling You: Why Women Hide the Whole Truth and What Marketers Can Do About It*) about what she learns. She also has written a column for *More* magazine and has been featured as the women's correspondent on CBS's *The Early Show*.

So...she's still a recovering yes-aholic. But she's made huge strides since her agency days. Now fifty-six, Mary Lou is writing to herself when she was operating at crisis speed every day.

Dear Marylou,

It's a Tuesday morning in May 1994. You are thirty-nine years old. You're sitting in the back of St. Patrick's Cathedral, sobbing—swaying in your seat like a distressed homeless person on a Manhattan sidewalk. A few minutes ago, you told a man who is a favorite boss and a friend that you were quitting your job to become president of another advertising agency.

Becoming one of the first females to reach that level before age forty should feel like a lifetime achievement. But instead of doing a dance of joy down Fifth Avenue, you're crying. Why? Because your decision made someone else unhappy. It's going to get worse when you walk out of this church hideout and tell your team that you're leaving. And it's killing you.

This is the biggest promotion of your life. Yet all you can think is: *How could I let everyone down? They'll be so hurt. Who will take care of them if I'm not there? Why did I have to be so selfish as to want this?*

Mary Lou, you are not in charge of everyone else's happiness. It's OK for you to worry if your mom and dad or your husband, Joe, or your brother, Jack, are happy. But not the people you work with—at least not all the time. They're not your family. Sometimes you will make personal choices that aren't so good for them. And when you walk out that door, you'll find that they go on and make their way without you.

Here's what I've learned. When you speak your heart and make changes and choices that are right for you, people understand. Maybe not right away, but they do. They're reminded that they need to make their own choices, too. Work can be uplifting and fulfilling, but over time it's inevitable that you'll wear out, you'll get stuck in a job that wastes your talents or compromises your values.

You've been a pleaser since you were a child. You love to believe that you can make it all better for everyone, that if only you say or do the right thing, you can fix it. How many times have you heard your mother saying, "Mary Lou, who left you in charge of making everyone happy?"

It will always be in your nature to want everyone to be OK. But you might cut a little slack for the girl in the mirror. What's the worst that could happen if you get comfortable asking for what you really want and need? They, whoever "they" are, may think less of you. But probably not. They may think you're not committed, or that you're selfish. But probably not.

Practice speaking your mind and risking that everyone won't always love you.

Now, start breathing. Stop crying. Walk back into that office and be happy for *yourself*. You've earned it.

Mary Lou

MEL ROBBINS
Host of the Syndicated Radio Show
The Mel Robbins Show

*Stop trying to prove how great you are to
the world, and just be you.*

———

MEL ROBBINS has morphed from lawyer to technology executive to life coach. And that was only the beginning. Today she is a fast-rising media star blending personal advice with entertaining commentary on hot topics on her daily talk-radio show, *The Mel Robbins Show*. She also interviews celebrities such as Barbara Walters, Donald Trump, and Bill Cosby on a show for Borders. Most recently, she left her position as a regular contributor on CNBC's *The Big Idea* with Donny Deutsch to become the host of a soon-to-be-unveiled prime-time reality series.

She describes herself as part cheerleader, part pain in the ass, part adviser, and part best friend, an amalgam of roles that suits a woman who wants to be the "Oprah of the airwaves." But this ambition took its time rising to the surface. For years Mel's direction was dictated by a powerful need for approval and the comforting sense of fortification that top credentials brought her.

The idea that these motivations might not be serving her well sneaked into her life when Mel, a beautiful, blonde go-getter, found herself at Boston College Law School. Always a worrier, Mel's anxiety began to mushroom into full-blown panic attacks during her first year. "I would wake up in the morning, my heart would be racing, and I would sense that something really bad was going to happen. As I lay there, with this foreboding sense of doom, I could feel the weight of it pushing me into the bed," she told me.

She would make herself get up in order to focus on something other than panic, get dressed, and drive to class, stopping at Dunkin' Donuts for a big cup of coffee but no breakfast. She smoked cigarettes at night, drank coffee in the morning, and endured panic attacks for three years. By the time she was in her third year of law school, Mel began to bring on attacks simply by worrying about whether she would get one. This "train wreck" of an experience, as Mel describes it, might have been avoided. Here, she writes to herself as a senior in high school in North Muskegon, Michigan, where she was an outstanding achiever headed for Dartmouth College.

Hello, Mel?

It's me, someone you don't know yet. I'm the real you. I'm buried so deep inside that you don't even know I'm

here. I'm so horribly out of focus that you wouldn't recognize me if I tapped you on the shoulder. I'm writing because you need me—sooner rather than later.

You're scratching your head. *What? I'm doing just fine,
thank you very much, whoever you are.* Yeah, you're the
school president. You're a tennis star. You've got top SAT
scores and you're headed to the Ivy League. You're the
girl with the big personality who walks in and takes over
the room.

But you're not in control and you're not happy—are
you? You ran for student-council president not because
you wanted to make an impact on your school, but because you wanted to be the one in charge rather than
someone who has no power. Now you worry about
whether your classmates like your decisions. You wonder
what people are saying about you. You fret about everything you do. You chug Mylanta before every tennis meet.
You are always afraid of "What if."

The king worry beneath it all is that you'd disappoint
people if they peeled back the accomplishments and saw
you for who you really are. You don't even know who you
are. You are just busy proving that you are the top dog.

You scurried to stack up achievements like boulders,
building a huge facade that looks pretty damn unassail-
able. But, notice. You can't take pleasure in any of it.
You seek these accomplishments so you can get praise.

Especially from your mom. You'll do anything to avoid that shift in her tone and energy—the one she uses when she's disappointed in you. Praise has motivated you since you were tiny.

Want to know why you're unhappy? It's simple, Mel. You are utterly disconnected from your authentic self. You've built yourself and this list of accomplishments simply to impress others. The reason you're always frantically worried that your facade of accomplishments will be knocked down is that it has no foundation that is truly connected to who *you* are.

What moves *you*? What thrills *you*—not your mother or your teachers? You can't answer those questions...yet.

I'm here to tell you there is something great waiting for you in the future. Something that fits you to a T. But you can't find it by desperately excelling at things you don't care about or focusing on proving to other people that you are great. You are great, Mel. You can have anything. As soon as you stop trying to prove how great you are to the world, and just be you, you will find both your power and your joy.

From the real Mel, finally.

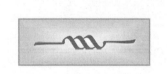

SYLVIE ROCHETTE
Founder and CEO of Victorian Epicure

To be really successful in life is to help others
succeed in their lives.

THE LETTER that Sylvie Rochette, one of Canada's foremost entrepreneurs, has written could be classified in the Be Careful What You Wish For Department. At thirty-seven, she decided she wanted to raise her kids, Amelia and Liam, herself, but also make enough money to have an income and send them to private school. So in 1991, she mixed up four spice dips, such as Lemon Dilly and Curry, and began selling them out of her station wagon at nearby farmers' markets and consumer trade shows.

From these simple jars, sold for $4.95 (Canadian), has sprung the fastest-growing direct-sales company in Canada: Epicure Selections. Like Tupperware or Pampered Chef, Epicure Selections markets and sells its products—fruit-dip mixes, salad-dressing mixes, sea-salt grinders, jellies, and some 300 seasoning blends—through in-home parties. More than 7,000 Epicure consultants across Canada helped

Victorian Epicure grow sales to over $40 million (Canadian) in 2009.

Today Sylvie's daughter, Amelia, works in the company as vice president of Epicure Selections. Liam is a dancer in Europe. Sylvie, whose politically active mother taught her children that to whom much is given, much is expected, is tackling education, poverty, and food security through the Epicure Foundation, which donates 5 percent of the company's pretax profits to Canadian charities. Her e-mail signature includes a quote: Dream big and make your journey count.

Pretty good for a business born out of a kitchen cabinet, right? Yes, but the most interesting part of this story is the paradox that Sylvie's success created. After several years of handling all sales and marketing, along with most other aspects of the business, herself, Sylvie in 1996 seized upon the idea of creating a direct-sales division. The decision instantly transformed the company's trajectory. Sales tripled from $300,000 to $900,000 in 1996 and then doubled for a couple of years after that.

Explosive growth further escalated the demands on Sylvie's time. "I found myself with children entering teenage-hood just as the company required more of me," she recalls, speaking with a delightful French accent by phone from British Columbia. "I had started the business to raise them myself, to be with them, and you have to be present to do that. At one point I thought of quitting altogether." Now fifty-five, Sylvie writes to herself at forty-one, when she needed to fortify herself against a daily drumbeat of guilt.

Dear Sylvie,

Right now your business is growing by leaps and bounds, but you can't help feeling terribly guilty that your children are being shortchanged. After all, you started Epicure to have a flexible schedule, to be with your kids. You have missed very few recitals, school plays, and field trips. You've been there at 3:15 to pick them up from school. But like everybody's, your day has twenty-four hours and Epicure does take you away physically and mentally.

To combat this corrosive feeling, it would be helpful to let go of some ideas and reframe others. Stop feeling pressure to lead a perfectly balanced life. No one walks around being balanced twenty-four hours a day. The concept of work-life balance makes for good articles and best-selling books, but it's a fallacy that undermines women.

Don't feel guilty that some aspect of your life is getting short shrift. If you do the best you can, it will be more than enough.

Here's the most persuasive proof I can offer. Years from now you will have a final conversation with your mother before she dies. You will mention your guilt about taking time away from your children. To your surprise, she will say she felt exactly the same way when she used to travel for political campaigns.

This is her gift to you. As a child you didn't feel short-changed. On the contrary, what you remember is how her adventures stimulated you.

So reframe your thinking. The traditional model children see is a parent working as an employee. But you are modeling determination, personal discipline, consistency, and making it on your own terms. Your children will also see you find answers to fascinating questions: How do you experience career success without forgoing relationships or suffering burnout? How do you gain the skills and confidence to create a holistic new kind of business? How do you make money while making a difference in the world?

And there is one thing that I deeply wish for: that your personal success represents collective success. The champagne and the Porsche are nice, but that measure of achievement only leads to more champagne and Porsches. No, to be really successful in life is to help others succeed in their lives.

Your journey counts,
Sylvie

CYNTHIA ROWLEY
Fashion Designer

Deny, defy, and sugarcoat.

———

CYNTHIA HAS LIKED to execute speedily on multiple fronts ever since she was a kid. Choosing a career in the notoriously brutal fashion industry has only intensified this trait. The dizzying ups and downs associated with launching her design business forced her to be resourceful and relentless.

"My accountant would tell me that my business had six months to live. I'd go into the bathroom, cry, and then figure out a way to keep it going," she remembers. Now that success has arrived, she doesn't dare relax. She explains: "Up until a certain point, I spent my entire career with people turning me down, people saying no. When you spend so long begging and hoping that someone will want your work, it's hard to turn opportunities away. Now we can take on only those that fit within a specific vision for our company."

Hence a surprisingly bountiful profusion of Cynthia Rowley products can be found across an array of markets.

The Cynthia Rowley collection includes women's ready-to-wear and accessories, and Cynthia has also designed beauty products, baby items, bicycles, active wear, shapewear, home-sewing patterns and tools, and much more. In addition to sixty Cynthia Rowley shops around the world (with a big concentration in Japan), Cynthia's clothes are sold in upscale stores such as Bergdorf Goodman and Saks, as well as online at sites like ShopBop. Cynthia has also written five books, most recently *Slim: A Fantasy Memoir* which includes her original drawings.

The eclectic sampler of work reflects Cynthia's exuberance and optimism. Her corporate bio reports "she enjoys many death-defying adventures, including surfing, water-skiing, and scuba diving."

Cynthia wanted to write to herself in 1994, after a decade of struggling to establish her business. At that point the direction of her personal life suddenly diverged dramatically in the opposite direction of her professional life. Tom Sullivan, her photographer husband of five years died after six months of illness from cancer. Two months after his death The Council of Fashion Designers recognized her with an award—her first from that influential organization.

"The moments that were the most monumental were always a mixed bag," Cynthia says. "He was my best friend. He was a very happy guy and completely at peace at the way his life turned out."

Dear Cynthia,

Three words: Don't look back.

Now more than ever, you need to get done what's right in front of you, while keeping in mind the big picture. Get it done. Then the next thing. And the next thing—steamroller style. Get your ideas out there, before someone else does.

Success is cumulative. It won't be one thing....It'll be the steady accumulation of massive amounts of effort. You know what they say—you're only as successful as your last collection.

Take this honor you've just been given as homage to Tom and his support of your career. He's pulling some strings up there for you. He's proud of you.

And never let go of your optimism. In the future your credo will be "deny, defy, and sugarcoat." That's another way to say "Don't take no for an answer." Deny the threats. Defy the odds. And sugarcoat the problems. It's just more fun that way.

Cheers,
Cynthia

SUZANNE SOMERS
Actress and Entrepreneur

We are not our accomplishments.

MANY PEOPLE know Suzanne Somers's name for only two reasons. They watched *Three's Company*, an enormously popular ABC sitcom in which she starred, or they saw an infomercial for ThighMaster, an exercise device that Suzanne tirelessly squeezed between her thighs. But the most interesting part of her story is the transition from one to the other—a changeover that has led to a versatile career, an array of businesses, and an improbable role as an outspoken health advocate.

We'll get to that transition. But first—are you ready?—take a look at Suzanne's surprising list of accomplishments. In addition to being an actress (her television credits include *Three's Company, She's the Sheriff, Step by Step, Candid Camera,* and *The Suzanne Somers Show*), a performer (she was named Las Vegas Female Entertainer of the Year in 1986, with Sinatra), and the author of nineteen books, including ten *New York Times* best sellers, Suzanne has established multiple businesses: a direct-sales company, SUZANNE; ThighMaster (more than 10 million sold); the Suzanne Somers Jewelry Collection (sold on ShopNBC); and lines of clothing, food, and skin- and hair-care products.

She learned to be resourceful at a young age, in self-defense. Her earliest memories are of hiding in the closet from her violent, alcoholic father—and cooking. "There was so much dysfunction in our house that dinner wasn't going to get made unless I made it. I made beef Stroganoff at age five," she remembers.

She felt ashamed when she got pregnant at eighteen and became a single mother. She dropped out of college and married the baby's father. After three years the marriage was over and money troubles began to dog Suzanne, particularly after a car seriously injured her son, Bruce, at age four. "I prayed. I had no money to pay for his bills. All my siblings were drunks or drug addicts. I was plagued by collection agencies," remembers Suzanne.

With the help of a generous therapist who charged $1 a visit, Suzanne slowly stabilized her life. By the time she was thirty she had begun to get work in commercials, but had decided to quit acting in favor of teaching cooking when in 1977 her agent persuaded her to go to one last audition for a television show. The show was *Three's Company* and she got the part.

Three's Company, in which Suzanne, Joyce DeWitt, and John Ritter played roommates whose lives were full of goofy adventures, was an immediate hit, ranking number one in the 1978–1979 season. No one seemed to realize that Suzanne spent two years utterly lost on the show. "I didn't know anything about acting. I just stared at John Ritter, trying to soak it in. Ritter was unbelievable," she says. "At the end of the second year, something changed. A bell went off in my head. I understood comedy was a rhythm. Then, in time, I started feeling like I deserved to be there, against all the odds."

During the show's fifth year Suzanne felt confident enough to ask to be paid substantially more—she requested a pay hike from $30,000 per show to $150,000. Male actors in leading shows were making $350,000 per show. "I thought, 'I have the number-one show and the highest demographic in all of TV. This isn't fair,'" she recalls.

The studio executives didn't agree, and Suzanne was fired amid a storm of publicity. Her fragile confidence shattered. She says: "I sat in my living room for a year, thinking 'Why did I do that?' I had the world by the tail and now I have nothing."

The letter below is from Suzanne today, at sixty-three, writing to that depressed thirty-five-year-old.

Dear Suzanne,

Who do you think you are? Why in the world did you think that you, *you of all people*, deserved to be on the number-one TV show in America and get a big fat raise for it?

You were sick of being kicked around your whole life—that's why. You finally managed to scrape together a little self-esteem after proving yourself. But you bumped up against a bunch of men who wanted to make an example of you. So they fired you for asking—just for asking!—to be paid what top male TV actors are getting.

OK, now what? I see that you've gone back to thinking you're worthless. You're thinking like the before-*Three's Company* Suzanne. You defined your success in terms of your accomplishment. And now that it's gone, you're back to being nothing.

As you sit there on the couch day after day, making yourself miserable, remember this: we are not our accomplishments. We can exist as worthy, lovable people with no accomplishments. True success means accepting yourself as you are.

Instead of focusing on what you lost, why don't you focus on what you have? You are Suzanne Somers.

Everyone in the country knows your name. What can you do with that?

Love,
Suzanne

KATE SPADE
Designer and Founder of Kate Spade

Being firm about your choices isn't pushy—
it's how to honor the gift inside you.

THE GIRL who used to beg her mom to drive her down to
Past Times, a vintage shop in Kansas City, Missouri, in order
to buy a little coat or a pair of gloves from the 1950s grew up
to become Kate Spade. The freshness of her designs in 1993,
when she and her husband, Andy Spade, started their company, stemmed from her ability to bring opposing qualities
together in one piece: elegance and whimsy, contemporary
and retro, spare geometry and rich color.

Maybe even more important, though, the small black
namesake label always conveyed good manners and whole-
someness. Can you imagine a Kate Spade bag featured in a
dark, brooding advertisement filled with pouting models?
Heavens to Betsy!

Kate herself trotted into her Park Avenue apartment
lobby, where I was waiting for her, looking exceptionally
fresh-faced and wholesome for a forty-seven-year-old.

Wearing blue running tights under athletic shorts and a light sweater, she had just come from a workout with her trainer. She probably would have loved a shower, but she brought me right up into her apartment.

The apartment was nothing like I expected, but I wanted to move in immediately. It has patrician bones—high ceilings, beautiful woodwork, huge rooms. But the decorating is free-handed and slightly bohemian. Large kilim-covered pillows lie in front of the fireplace. Art of all kinds fills the walls in the long foyer and living room. Not much wall space is left. Kate and Andy clearly had fallen in love with all these pieces and just kept putting them up wherever they found a spot. The mix of styles, colors, and media gave me the feeling that a lively conversation was happening in that room even when no one was present.

Exercise—not to mention being home in the middle of a Thursday afternoon—was still a novelty for Kate. She, Andy, and their two partners had sold Kate Spade (the company) eighteen months prior to our meeting and completed the transition six months after that.

"I was always so crazy busy that putting exercise into the schedule… I just didn't do it," she said with a husky chuckle. The agenda these days is play dates, baking muffins, and taking four-year-old Bea to nursery school, Kate explained as we settled down on a couch in the living room with Henry, Kate's arthritic Maltese, between us. Bea was taking her nap. "I'm having a ball," she said. "I'm still waiting for the regret. Maybe it's my Catholic upbringing. You know, I could *not* have made the right decision, could I?"

It could have easily been more traumatic. Kate and Andy, who had dated at Arizona State University, began interweaving marriage, friendships, and personal expression with their business just after they turned thirty. Kate made her first square handbag pattern out of construction paper in 1992. Andy didn't quit his job until 1996. The couple had so much inventory stacked in their 1,800–square foot Tribeca loft in 1997 that they had a path from the bedroom to the bathroom. Even after they sold 56 percent of the company to Neiman Marcus for $33.6 million in 1999, the Spades and partners Elyce Arons and Pamela Bell were free to run and expand the company as they chose.

Yet when Neiman Marcus's owners decided to sell the operation—necessitating the sale of its ownership in Kate Spade and Laura Mercier—it didn't take too long for the Spades and their partners to recognize that they were ready to sell the remaining 44 percent stake and leave the company. Liz Claiborne became Kate Spade's new owner.

"It was an intensely personal decision. It wasn't the idea of working with the new owner that we didn't like. Liz Claiborne was a great person who started a great company. It's just that our identities were so embedded in the Kate Spade company," Kate explained. "How would it be to have that mind-set and stay on, once someone else owned the company? It would have been a lot to ask."

Kate chose to write to her younger self during the 1993 to 2000 time period, when she was establishing and growing the now world-famous brand.

Dear Katy,

Unlike most people, you have no trouble hearing what your gut has to say. The connection between your instincts and your brain is loud and clear. For any given decision—whether it's the length of a strap on a new bag or an advertising campaign—your reaction is visceral.

When you feel a rush, a sense of excitement that is both physical and mental, it's a YES.

If the sensation is like "ugh" in your gut, an impression of something wrong, the answer is NO.

This communion with your intuition is part of your creative gift. It's so baked into the way you, Andy, and your partners are growing up together in the business that sometimes you're not even aware of it. And that's the first thing I want to tell you: this is your best tool. It's like a divining rod—not easily explained, but capable of enchanting feats.

Stick with these gut reactions a little more. When someone opposes your instincts, especially if they are passionate about it, you back down too often. Occasionally the sales department can talk you into adding certain styles to a line, even though you may feel they're superfluous. Or, sometimes you second-guess your instinct to say "no" about an advertising campaign.

To you it seems that winning the decision isn't worth alienating or offending someone. But you shouldn't let yourself be talked out of your point of view. And when you feel things are going in the wrong direction, speak up.

Of course you, Katy Brosnahan, were brought up to be nice. And boy, are you! Remember how grateful you were when you hired your first employees? Yep, you practically fell all over yourself to get *them* coffee! This is absolutely part of who you are. You'll never be Donald Trump, barking out orders, just like you'll never have long legs. (Sorry, even in the future that never happens...)

Still, you most definitely need to be OK with people disagreeing with you—or even disliking your decisions. This is an aptitude you'll want to develop in your daughter someday. By then you'll understand that being firm about your choices isn't pushy—it's how to honor the gift inside you.

With confidence in your intuition,
Katy

LISA STONE
Co-Founder of BlogHer

*Ultimately your success will be rooted in
your heart, not in your brain.*

———

BLOGHER is the foremost hub of female bloggers. It exists in the virtual world, drawing millions of online visitors. But the community also vibrates with life in the real world, at BlogHer's annual conference. The Internet pioneer who co-founded BlogHer in 2005 with two partners (Elisa Camahort Page and Jory Des Jardins) is Lisa Stone, who is also the first Internet journalist to be awarded a Nieman Fellowship by Harvard University.

She loves to work, at times to her detriment. Prior to BlogHer, Lisa helped launch three sponsored blogging networks, was editor in chief/vice president of programming for women.com, and launched online networks and programming for magazines at Hearst and Rodale as well as for E! Television/Online and Bloomberg.

How did she do it? "I learned I'm an absolutist. I didn't have a beer for two years. I slept only two or three hours at night. I will always have a lifelong struggle with workaholism," she says.

This tsunami of productivity followed a dramatic break with her old life. In 1997, when she was thirty, she had a solid career as a journalist, a one-year-old, and a failing marriage. At the same time, she was intensely disillusioned with the news industry. "I couldn't stand the level of intellectual patronization," she remembers.

She might have lived with the professional frustration and the personal hell of a bad marriage if it weren't for her son, Jake. "Being a mother really sparked my ability to believe in myself. He needed a mom who was as excited about life as he was," says Lisa.

So she left her husband and her job, dumbfounding everyone around her. She had no plan, and wasn't even sure how she'd put groceries on the table. Now forty-three, Lisa writes to herself in October 1997.

Lisa,

Leaving the traditional newsroom and your husband in the same year blew everyone's minds. Yours included. You knew you couldn't stay. But, now, where to go?

You've done the right thing. Today is the beginning of the end of trying to please people by saying everything is *just fine* even when you know it so isn't (as your tweenage son will say in 2008). Today, his influence is just beginning. Look into his beautiful baby face to see who gave you the strength to do what was right, for him and for you. You finally got angry about the way you were allowing yourself to be treated. For him you stood up for what you think is right. It won't be the last time.

You don't know it yet, but motherhood just jettisoned your ability to sit on the sidelines and wait for someone else to rescue you—with ideas, income, or inspiration. You'll never again be able to act against your own good opinions to keep the peace at home or at work.

The result? You'll love new-media start-ups, where your tolerance for tension and stress can be a good thing. By leaving reporting and unchaining yourself from a desk, you'll not only become the mother you want to be, but you'll be forced to experiment. You'll develop new business models to support Web writers. You'll help raise millions of dollars to fund a company to create opportunities for other women (and men!) to write the kind of news missing from today's journalism. You'll love your work.

But there's one thing I wish I could save you from: the loneliness and self-imposed isolation that will send you into a major depression in five years. Single motherhood is hard, but you're using it to build a deflector shield for human emotion. No dice. Ultimately your success will be rooted in your heart, not in your brain. You'll fight that at first, and try to turn yourself into a binary automaton who only works and mothers, rather than feels. As if.

The price? As you blossom creatively, you will also bottom out emotionally because you are so lonely. The result will be a yearlong writer's block and a real crisis. One day, your sisters and your best friends will tell you it's time to stop that and go talk to the professionals. Listen to them. Get help. Stop isolating yourself and start sharing what's really on your mind with your family and friends. That way, when a hot computer nerd and single father comes along, you'll be ready to start living again.

Go get 'em.

Lisa

HANNAH STORM
Co-Host of ESPN's *SportsCenter*

Stop worrying. It's useless.

———

HANNAH STORM was the first female anchor as host of CNN's *Sports Tonight* from 1989 to 1992. Such breakthroughs are fun while they're happening, but also incredibly challenging and stressful. Hannah remembers the pressure and the sense of living in a mercilessly transparent fishbowl. "Every time I messed up I would get mail. They even talked about how I dressed. There would be questions about why the network was allowing a woman to cover sports," she says.

All of that was intensified by a daily concern: a port-wine stain birthmark below her left eye, sort of a permanent black eye. Hannah says she was terribly self-conscious about it as a kid who moved frequently with her family. (Her father is Mike Storen, who was commissioner of the American Basketball Association and president of the Atlanta Hawks in the NBA.) People would ask awkward questions: "What happened to your face?" "Were you hit in the eye?" In high school, she covered the mark with heavy makeup and was reluctant to go swimming with friends because the camouflage would wash off.

To pursue a career in an image-conscious, visual industry with a disfigurement was daunting. Yet she did not let it limit her. She moved from CNN to NBC in 1992, becoming the first female network studio host of a major sports property, hosting Major League Baseball games from 1994 to 2000 and *The NBA on NBC* from 1997 to 2002, among many other duties. Then she hopped over to CBS and became a host on *The Early Show*, before joining ESPN in 2008 to launch the new daytime *SportsCenter*.

Hannah's birthmark now means something different to her. "I realized you don't have to be perfect, even in such a visually oriented field. And I feel blessed because this has given me an understanding for others, no matter what they are self-conscious about," she says. In 2008, she started the Hannah Storm Foundation, which raises money for medical treatment for children born with vascular birthmarks. More than one in ten infants are affected, and the condition can be life-threatening. Often, corrective surgeries are not covered by insurance.

Her birthmark is not the focus of Hannah's letter to her younger self, although it ties in to the central topic: worrying. This pedestrian-sounding activity began to suck up a lot of Hannah's emotional energy in high school, when she would lie in bed at night framing and reframing her concerns, attempting to assuage her self consciousness. Says Hannah: "It's a control thing. You want to control the situation, whatever it is."

She occasionally sees the eldest of her three daughters subjecting herself to the same mental torture. It reminds Hannah of how much she has learned about regulating anxiety. Now forty-seven, she is addressing herself in her late twenties, when she began working at CNN.

Dear Hannah,

Stop the worrying. It's useless.

The part of you that works so hard—that wants so badly to be perfect—has served you well. How else could you progress in this all-male industry where your every word (even your outfits!) is so closely scrutinized?

But your desire for controlling the circumstances around you is in overdrive. Here you are, in the bathroom—your Inner Sanctum of Worry—confronting your detractors in the mirror. The shower, where it's quiet, and your bed at night are where the thoughts and worries start piling up. Your mind is like an organ trying to digest the day's hard lumps, nudging them over to one side, then the other, attempting to smooth out the knots. It chews and chews. It collects new anxieties about tomorrow. The lumps grow bigger and bigger. Till finally...what?

Nothing. Worrying doesn't make one whit of difference to the things that happened that day or will happen the next. It just ruins your sleep.

It's time to starve the ravenous beast. First, catch yourself in the act of worrying. Second, learn to distinguish between what you can't control and what you can. Don't make assumptions about anything. Finally, most important of all, rewrite the script you use when you talk to yourself about what happens. Put a positive spin on the day's events...and those to come.

A producer yells at you? Say, "Wow. Isn't he in a bad mood today?" rather than "Oh my goodness, what did I do wrong?"

Lean on your faith too, like you always have. Remember the passage from Phillipians: "Don't worry about anything; instead pray about everything. Tell God what you need and thank Him for everything."

Before you leave in the morning don't forget to glance at that little saying taped up in the bathroom.

"Good morning, this is God.

I'll be handling all your problems today. I will not need your help—so have a nice day."

With peace of mind,
Hannah

C. Vivian Stringer
Women's Basketball Coach at Rutgers University

*You have to work hard to find ways to integrate
your work with your family.*

As THE ELDEST of six kids in the Stoner family, C. Vivian
Stringer grew up amid high expectations. Her parents gave
their kids a long list of chores, held family meetings after
church every Sunday, and expected excellence in academics
and athletics in keeping with Stoner tradition. That her father, Buddy, was a coal miner and that money was often
tight were inconsequential next to her father's joyous
music-making and her mother, Thelma's, masterful people-
management skills.

"Just to see my mom and dad smile was a joy. I always
wanted to do things to make them happy and proud,"
Coach Stringer told me. Her father was a key example in
two of her largest life lessons. When she was in high school
her father had to have both of his legs amputated up to his
knees. Instead of collecting disability, he took a job in the
mine office. Instead of complaining about the pain, when

people asked how he was, he'd laugh and say: "I'm kicking, but not too high."

He was also the one who encouraged her to stand up for what was right at a young age. A gifted neighborhood athlete, V.I., as she was called, had no opportunity to play organized sports at school. But she figured being a cheerleader was one way to get onto the courts and fields. She practiced, thought she'd nailed every cheer at the tryouts, and was upset that she didn't make the squad. She never even noticed that all of the girls who did were white, as they had been during the entire history of German Township High School (with one exception, when Vivian was in elementary school).

The head of a local chapter of the NAACP visited her house to ask Vivian to protest the decision, along with another talented black athlete who had not made the cut. Predictably, Vivian shied away from the inevitable negative repercussions she foresaw and said, "No."

Her father spoke to her thoughtfully before she went to bed that night, pointing out that her choice affected not only her, but also future generations of deserving young women. As she recounts in her book, *Standing Tall*, he also said, "There comes a point in your life when you must stand, because if you don't stand for something, you'll fall for anything. I want you to think seriously about giving, because you are the one who can." She agreed to allow the

NAACP to present her and the other black girl to the school board, which allowed the girls to became part of the cheerleading squad.

Shaped by such strong familial forces and propelled by her own excitement about coaching, Coach Stringer has put together a stunning record of achievement in nearly four decades of coaching. She was the first coach—male or female—in NCAA history to lead three different women's programs to the NCAA Final Four: Cheyney State College in 1982 (now Cheyney University of Pennsylvania), the University of Iowa in 1993, and Rutgers University in 2000 and 2007. She has been named National Coach of the Year three times by her peers and was inducted into the Women's Basketball Hall of Fame in 2001 and the Naismith Memorial Basketball Hall of Fame in 2009.

Her ambitions for her players are far broader than the basketball court, though. That she succeeds is evident in many ways, but her impact was particularly visible in April 2007 after radio talk-show host Don Imus used a racial slur to describe the Rutgers team. The dignity with which Coach Stringer and her players responded was testimony to their strength of character.

"My dream for the young ladies I coach is that they never measure themselves with someone else's yardstick, or simply by wins and losses. I would like them to know that real success is achieved when you set your own worth, fulfill your own destiny, and stand up for what you know to be right," says Vivian.

Her achievements have not insulated her from personal tragedy. Her daughter, Janine (called Nina) contracted spinal meningitis when she was fourteen months old. Her husband, Bill, who was her college sweetheart and a stalwart believer in his wife, had a fatal heart attack when he was forty-seven, leaving Vivian a single mother of Nina, David, and Justin. Vivian's letter is written to herself in 1981, before those tragedies.

Dear V.I.,

The books tell you not to mix pleasure with work. Not to mix family and friends with your professional life. You're trying to be the consummate coach. But Vivian, when your profession is as demanding as coaching, you have to work hard to find ways to integrate your work with your family. The days that you've already lost are gone forever. Life dictates that we will always work hard but with that said, you must also live. What is life, if it is just work? What makes us happy? Your family, husband, children, parents, sisters and brothers are that for you.

You're riding in a bus with the team as you always do. Bill and the kids are following you in the car, as they always do. Think of how many hours they have ridden—and will ride—without you sitting beside them. It's a small thing, but that is time you could be with them that wouldn't hurt your team. You never know when that loved person won't be available to be with you. As much as you can, remember that the most important reasons for existing and living are the people you love, who care about you so deeply. Your family. Your husband. Open your eyes and ears for the chances to be with them even more.

When Bill suggests going away out west with the kids for a week, do it. Yes, you could spend that week preparing for a clinic you'll be holding for elementary-school kids. But it's time to recognize that you know what you can do very well by now. You don't need to prepare with the same intensity because you've grown and developed so much expertise. You're not at risk of losing the skills and reputation you've created as a coach if you ease up just a little.

And, as life goes on, hold on to a critical distinction. What you do is not who you are.

Again: what you do is *not* who you are.

You are a hall-of-fame coach in the making, but, really, you are a human being. A woman who likes to goof around, listen to jazz music, and dance. You're a mom. You're a wife. If you let what you do professionally define you completely, you won't know who you are and you'll be disappointed tremendously in life.

Slow down a little and enjoy life. Don't deny yourself that. It would be OK if you went to some movies. It would be fine if you didn't study and work so very, very hard. You'll look back on the times you brought Justin and David to Saturday-morning practices with you as some of the best times ever. You'll feel at peace during times like those. Make more of those moments happen.

With compassion and abiding love,
Vivian

Trudy Sullivan
CEO and President of The Talbots

You can't take failure personally.

If you ever get the chance to meet Trudy Sullivan, take a good look at what she's wearing! This is a woman with impeccable fashion credentials. She has been president of J.Crew and Liz Claiborne and is now president and CEO of The Talbots, where—you may have noticed—she is seriously shaking things up.

Trudy started her work life in Boston as a buyer for Jordan Marsh. She knew she wanted to start her own business, so after seven years there, she moved to Filene's, where she could learn how to manage and run stores. She liked it better than she expected. Another seven years went by.

By 1985 Trudy had been married for eleven years and was ready to take the plunge as an entrepreneur. She had a really great idea for a chain of stores carrying fashion in larger sizes. At the time, this was a neglected backwater filled with frumpy clothes. Trudy put all her savings into her venture—which was called T. Deane—and it was a sensational hit. She opened three stores in Wellesley, Massachusetts, and attracted $7 million in venture-capital money, which enabled her to expand to twenty-two stores.

Just in case starting and rapidly growing a chain of stores was not intense enough for Trudy, life handed her a couple of surprises. The first occurred two months after she launched T. Deane: she discovered she was pregnant. "When you're the principal you can bring the baby to work with you," she told me. "Often, she would sleep in a basket under my desk for the first five or six weeks."

The second surprise was baby number two, who came along two years later. By the time T. Deane had been under way for three-and-a-half years, Trudy's husband had left his position at Wang Laboratories, where he was responsible for IR and PR, and joined her in the business—and Trudy was just about to complete another round of raising venture capital.

Then . . . disaster. While Trudy was building her business, the financial world was convulsed by recession. Campeau Corporation of Canada took over Federated Department Stores after a bidding war, loading it up with so much debt that Federated could not pay interest on the loans. This failure, along with economic conditions in general and in the retail sector in particular, extinguished investors' interest in retail. Within weeks it became clear that Trudy would not be able to get funding and had no other choice but to close her fledgling company.

Now sixty, Trudy is writing to herself at thirty-nine, when she shut down T. Deane.

Dear Trudy,

As you close T. Deane it feels like you are closing the door on yourself. You put everything you had into this. You prepared by getting the right work experience for fourteen years. You invested your treasure. Even the birth of your family could not keep you from the launch of your business.

And what will you have to show for it? Nothing.

That's what you feel right now, and I can't blame you. A sense of failure is scalding your heart.

Trudy, here's the fast way to get through this. Understand that the fact that your business didn't work doesn't mean that you're dumb or that you're a failure. You can't allow the failure of T. Deane to affect your self-worth. The real lesson here is that you can't take failure personally. It is simply a signal that God has other plans.

This may seem impossible to believe right now, but in fact you have already learned to correct your course while running T. Deane. No other conventional job in retailing would have exposed you to such a broad array of responsibilities in such a short time period. Think about it.

When you ran into problems you often had to detach, step back, reassess, and try something different. This is what successful people do. Unsuccessful people stay stuck, trying to solve a problem the same way, day after day, even if their approach isn't working. And some people never even try in the first place!

So, left foot, right foot—keep moving, Trudy. Don't over-invest emotionally in what happened. Don't let your fears betray your hopes. And don't feel guilty.

Turn the page; the future awaits.

Trudy

LINDA KAPLAN THALER
Author and Founder of
The Kaplan Thaler Group

Your gut has an IQ of 100,000.

THERE AREN'T MANY women business leaders brave enough to wear their femininity on their sleeves . . . at their offices and on their book jackets. Linda Kaplan Thaler does. She runs The Kaplan Thaler Group, a billion-dollar Manhattan advertising and entertainment company, which she founded in 1997, with an unapologetic dose of estrogen.

One of her best-known commercials is the orgasmic "Yes! Yes! Yes!" shampoo-and-shower vignette for Herbal Essences. She also composed the "I Don't Wanna Grow Up, I'm a Toys'R'Us Kid" jingle and the "Kodak Moments" concept. Her company created the Aflac duck commercials, among many others, collecting thirteen CLIOs and a raft of other awards along the way. Her most recent book is *The Power of Nice: How to Conquer the Business World with Kindness,* which she co-wrote with Robin Koval.

When she entered her midtown office, where we spoke, this powerhouse looked adorable, with long hair, big round eyes, and eyelash-tangling bangs. She's disarmingly open, a great storyteller and likes to laugh. She'd be the friend who'd loan you her new, unworn designer outfit for the event where you absolutely have to look smashing.

The key to Linda's success, she says, was tied to the sad period of time when she was desperately trying to get pregnant. After she got married at the "ripe old age of thirty-six," she thought she'd have a couple of babies, no problem. "Not only did I have trouble getting pregnant, I went through some unfortunate miscarriages. I was approaching forty and still had not been able to start a family," she remembers.

Around this time, a doctor discovered a lump in Linda's breast. She had breast cancer at thirty-nine. After a mastectomy, her doctors were in conflict about wheter or not it was safe for her to have children. She remembers: "I had this brief respite. My surgeon told me, 'You're going to live.' But it was followed by, 'But you are not going to be able to conceive.' I went through a year where I wanted to get pregnant, but if I got pregnant I was afraid I might die."

She began seeing a hypnotherapist while struggling with her predicament. As she mourned and gradually accepted that she would not be able to get pregnant, she started repeating a specific date—May 22—while under hypnosis at her sessions. The therapist asked, "What's May 22?" Linda said she didn't know but that she thought she might get pregnant on May 22. Months passed. The day came. Even though most women ovulate around the 14th day of their cycle, Linda woke up on the 22nd day of her cycle (in May) certain that she and her husband would be able to conceive a child that very day.

She was forty-one. She was alive. And she *did* become pregnant, all of which elated her. The baby, Michael, now eighteen, became a three-time national chess champion at the elementary-school level. Three years after he was born, Linda gave birth to Emily, now fifteen. The cancer did not return.

Linda, who is now fifty-nine, writes to her younger self about the unlikely business lesson that emerged from her intense desire to have children and her bout with cancer.

Dear Linda,

For twenty years you've been writing award-winning ad campaigns but you still have never quite felt like you've made it. Yes, you wrote the Toys"R"Us song and helped America experience Kodak moments. But somehow you still don't feel like you've earned the accolades that have come your way.

But you learned something so counterintuitive, yet so true while you were trying and failing to have kids.

When you accept that you may fail, you can do anything. The trick is to think of failure as impersonal. It doesn't attach itself to you. It's transitory. It passes through. If you can think of failure this way, you will rob it of its power to immobilize you. Failing is not a life or death situation, but cancer sure is. Having it at such a young age made you stronger, although you may not realize that yet. If you try something and fail, you can live with that. Trust me.

Better yet, now that you're not afraid to fail, you'll never be afraid of taking risks. You'd never have considered starting your own company before this struggle. But now you have and it will become more successful that you ever dreamed possible.

You've also learned something else. When you were at your darkest moment, you thought nothing could get better. Now you know that while you don't have control over what life is going to do to you, you do have control over your perspective. So don't be myopic about where you are in your life at any given moment.

Finally, respect your body's physical wisdom. Your conscious brain is the size of your computer screen. It can only hold so much. But your gut has an IQ of 100,000. Trust it. The body knows things in our gut before we know them in our head. You listened to your body saying, "May 22." It was right and the doctors were wrong. You chose to lose the fear and in return you gained so much.

So take that bold new business step, and keep on walking!

Proudly,
Linda

DIANE VON FURSTENBERG
Fashion Designer and Founder of DVF

Don't fight your destiny, but keep your character.

———

MEETING DIANE von Furstenberg had a delusory effect on me. Little did I know how extensively her image and her brand had affixed themselves to my brain. These impressions were so strong that when I encountered an authentic Warhol poster of DVF, for example, or Diane herself, in the flesh, a sensation of unreality crept over me, as if they were counterfeit.

My real-life DVF immersion started when I bought one of her iconic wrap dresses to wear to my meeting with Diane. The saleswoman, probably in her twenties, said: "When you meet her, please thank her from women everywhere that we can put on one of her dresses and feel like a lady."

Properly outfitted, I wear the dress on a rainy June afternoon when I step into the ultrahip lobby of DVF's design studio. A narrow stretch of water runs along one side of the space, fronted by a bench sporting fuchsia upholstery. A Cinderella staircase descends in the center and the famous Warhol prints of Diane with one arm raised over her head are everywhere. After he died she bought up every piece of art he had made using her image except for one poster that hangs in Pittsburgh's Warhol Museum.

A bevy of young women is meeting amid fabric swatches and notebooks just outside Diane's enormous penthouse office. There is not a speck of cubicle ambiance to be found here. Downstairs is slick and modern. Upstairs is contemporary meets *Out of Africa* meets *The King and I*. Animal-print rugs are layered on the floor. A large Buddha bust, Balinese accents, and furniture from all over the globe make Diane's office feel like a living room rather than a workplace.

We sit on a modern daybed. Diane sinks fluidly down onto one end, tucking her shins under her like the devoted yoga student that she is. It's tempting to describe her as cat-like because of these slinky movements, so unexpected in a sixty-three-year-old. But it's Diane's brown-eyed, 1,000-yard gaze—lazy and penetrating at the same time—that seems most feline. "I feel exactly the same as when I was a little girl, absolutely the same," she says with a rich French accent, about looking back at her younger self. "Yes, you learn. Yes, sometimes you're less or more insecure. But I feel pretty much the same."

You probably know the fairy-tale part of Diane's story: She was the Belgian who married a prince (Eduard Egon von und zu Fürstenberg) at twenty-three, built a multimillion-dollar business on the jersey back of a universally flattering wrap dress, adorned a cover of *Newsweek*, and hobnobbed with Manhattan's beautiful people, such as *Vogue* editor Diana Vreeland, designer Halston, artist Andy Warhol, and jewelry designer Elsa Peretti—all by the time she was thirty years old.

Her comeback, after living in Paris from 1983 to 1989, was equally remarkable. Those five years had seriously compromised her brands, which she had licensed to other companies. Royalties had amounted to $4 million annually back in 1983. By the time she returned they'd dropped by 75 percent. Product quality and distribution had deteriorated badly.

She began successfully selling a new line of silk dresses on QVC in 1992. A decade after selling the trademark for her fragrance and beauty business for $22 million she bought it back for $250,000. In 1994 she survived cancer at the base of her tongue and in her soft palate. Three years later she started Diane von Furstenberg, the fashion company, which had sales of about $200 million in 2009. In 2001 she married media mogul Barry Diller.

There's a little-appreciated explanation for her multiple business successes and personal accomplishments, which Talita, Diane's blond haired ten year old granddaughter, supplies as she sidles up to her grandmother during our talk. Diane asks Talita what she might write about in a letter to *her*self at five years old.

Talita: Not to be scared of spiders.

Diane: Spiders. What are they going to do?

Talita: They bite you.

Diane: My mother didn't allow me to be afraid. If I was afraid of the dark she would have locked me in the closet. After a half hour you realize there is nothing to be afraid of.

Me: Your mother sounds very strong.

Talita: She passed through a concentration camp.

Diane's mother, Lily Nahmias, was twenty-one and weighed forty-nine pounds when she was freed from a German concentration camp in 1945. One of the key beliefs she brought out of that experience was this: what may seem to be the absolute worst thing to happen to you can in fact be the best. She also learned the crucial importance of being self-sufficient. "In my family we would not want anything for our child except for them to be in control of their own life. That's the only thing that matters," Diane says.

Diane writes to herself at twenty-three, not long after she had apprenticed herself to Angelo Ferretti, a man in his forties who owned a knitting and printing plant in Como, Italy.

Dear Diane,

Yes, you are pregnant. And no, you didn't want to be. But you followed your mother's advice and told Egon. He's your fiancé, she pointed out. You can't just go have Dr. S. take care of this without telling Egon that you are carrying his child. And now he's replied by telegram:

No question of S. Marriage will occur the 15th of July. Organize it as rapidly as possible. I rejoice. Thinking of you. Love and kisses, Eduard Egon.

You always wanted to be a certain kind of woman. Independent, glamorous, and on your own. Now your ideal is in jeopardy. A baby and a marriage are coming. You believe you have learned absolutely nothing from Angelo. How will you ever become your own person?

I tell you now: you can. The things you have learned during these past few months are seeds that will flower in your future. Jersey. Printing. Coloring. Patternmaking. They are all you will need.

Marriage and a baby feel like a threat to your dreams of independence, especially financial independence. But the threat will push you to make some patterns and samples to take to America to try to sell. In a few months you will cross an ocean on a boat with a baby in your stomach and samples in your trunk, planning your future in your head. It won't be easy, but in the end the one thing that you thought would prevent your independence from happening—the fact that you are pregnant—will force it all to happen faster.

The message is: don't fight your destiny, but keep your character.

Success is being coherent with who you are.

With great respect,
DVF

Barbara Walters
Co-Executive Producer and Co-Host of *The View*

If you do what you love, you will be successful.

———

Her exclusive—and often first-ever—interviews with world leaders, movie stars, and newsmakers around the globe have made Barbara Walters an instantly familiar television icon. Question by carefully thought-out question, Barbara has led millions of us into the hearts and minds of heroes, villains, and tabloid fixtures. It's easy to forget that it took time, hard work, and a pioneering spirit to earn the right to sit in her upholstered interviewer's chair.

Regarding her letter about what she knows now about success, she says: "It isn't that I didn't know all of these things on my unsteady climb up the ladder. I just never thought about them. I was too busy working. But looking back, this is what I now know that I wish I had known earlier."

Dear Barbara,

Here is the truth. Here is the secret to success. If you follow your bliss, if you do what you love, you will be successful, at least in your own terms. And your own terms are the most important.

Arrive early to work and stay late.

Don't whine.

Don't blame others.

Compliment whenever possible.

Fight the big fights only.

Remember that the person you are putting down today may be your boss tomorrow.

Remember, too, that there is a difference between a job and a career, and a career often means sacrifices.

Have a private life. Cherish your friends, especially the ones who you know will cherish you even if, or when, you are no longer a success.

Failure, if you learn from it, can lead to success.

Success is wonderful. But read the above again. It isn't everything.

It cannot be said enough: follow your bliss.

Barbara

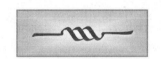

Suzy Welch
Author and Columnist

*Every journey takes you outside your comfort
zone and away from what is familiar—
if it is a journey worth taking.*

WHEW! YOU'D think Suzy Welch would show a few signs of
fatigue. She is not only the mother of four and wife to former GE chairman Jack Welch, she has also been on a wildly
productive streak. She and Jack have written *Winning: The
Answers* as well as "The Welch Way," a popular *BusinessWeek*
column. They are soon set to launch an online MBA program
at Chancellor University that will offer Jack Welch's celebrated business philosophy in an innovative online curricu-
lum. Suzy also writes a column for *O, The Oprah Magazine*
and contributes to the culture and politics Web site *The Daily
Beast*. Her latest book is *10-10-10: A Life-Transforming Idea*.

The fifty-year-old who opened the door flashed me a big
smile and had energy to spare. Suzy's 46th-floor Manhattan apartment made everything in the distant city below
feel calm and manageable. In the midst of a fifteen-city

tour for *10-10-10*, Suzy had been on Don Imus's radio show earlier that morning. The book had previously hit number five on the *New York Times*'s list of best-selling business books, and now, demonstrating the Imus show's impact, its Amazon ranking fell steadily as we talked.

10-10-10 was born out of a fraught period in Suzy's life that may sound familiar. In her thirties and torn by perpetually competing family and work demands, she found that she often made choices haphazardly, based on gut instinct or even plain old guilt. The tool she devised for herself to counter this dynamic is simple but penetrating: assess a decision by how your choice will affect your life in 10 minutes, 10 months, and 10 years and then—most importantly—bring your own personal values to bear on the choice.

Before she invented this three-layer sieve, Suzy says, "I made many of my decisions as if I were watching them from a moving car. My life was living me. I wasn't living my life." Small wonder. Along with raising her children in her thirties, she also worked as a management consultant before ascending the editorial ladder at the *Harvard Business Review*, where she eventually became editor in chief. The frenzied activity, she now says, was meant to fill an emotional black hole at the center of her life.

It's hard to imagine this comfortable, charismatic woman ever feeling lost and worthless. But as she juggled motherhood, work, and an unraveling marriage, she often found herself frantically scrambling to please everyone at once, and automatically saying "yes" to everything that came her way—regardless of the consequences.

Now happily married to Jack, Suzy says her past taught her how hard—and ultimately how transformative—it is to live a values-driven life, building your joy decision by decision. Her letter is written to herself when she was a twenty-three-year-old reporter at the *Miami Herald*.

Dear Suzy,

Hey, remember the time you told everyone, "I just can't wait to throw my career out the window, settle down and get married, and then go live in a Victorian fixer-upper with a white picket fence in the suburbs?"

Yeah, you know, I don't remember that either. In fact, I sort of remember you telling everyone, "*Oh, God, I wanna be Oriana Fallaci*" instead.

I remember because every time you made that claim—and you made it a lot—you annoyed people; surely you recall that too, don't you? Your family certainly thought it was OK for you to want to be a foreign correspondent. They got the coolness quotient of that gig—the travel, the writing, the freedom and excitement of it all. "But why," they would always ask, "do you want to be the most over-the-top member of the breed? Why do you want to live that close to the edge?"

You would answer: "Is there someplace better to live?" And you know, Suzy, you sounded pretty sure of yourself when you said that.

That's why I'm sort of curious about those suitcases on your living-room floor.

I know, I know—home beckons. You ache for Boston's familiarity far more than you ever expected. You miss your sisters; Della's loyalty, Elin's steadfastness. You miss your friends, the ones who laugh their heads off at Monty Python like you do and want to go out for sushi every Friday night too. You miss the crooked streets you know so well; you miss never getting lost and thinking, "Holy shit, I'm in deep trouble." You miss the ease. The comfort. I understand; who wouldn't?

Over the last two years Miami has never offered you that ease, that comfort. And at first, oh, what a kick that was. You arrived at twenty-one, on your own. Instantly, you could feel the promise; the city was wild and unruly, and in its mystery, darkly glamorous.

You could have just as easily been in Bogotá or Rio in those early days. The streets were exploding with drug violence and race rioting. The days were thrilling and tumultuous; the stories blew through the newsroom like little hurricanes. And at night in the bars and restaurants you reporters stuck together in a pack while the Cubans who owned the city, regal, haughty, and unknowable, considered you with cool curiosity and you considered them back—with a desperation to be let in.

You thought that you'd stay forever. Or at least until you could find a way to an assignment someplace farther away and even closer to the edge.

But then, imperceptibly, the homesickness started to creep in, and the longing too—for love, I guess. A desire for people who would say, "Come in. You're one of us." A Valentine's Day came and went without even a hint of romance, and then another. A few friends from the newsroom moved away, back up north. A boss was jerking you around more and more.

And then one day, the letter arrived. You know which one I'm talking about. The one from the old boyfriend saying, "When are you coming home?"

Look, every journey—every daring leap we make—has its tough patches. Its hours of loneliness, its days and nights of doubt. Every journey takes you outside your comfort zone and away from what is familiar—if it is a journey worth taking.

You've spent your whole life up until now wanting to lead a life of your own making. Yearning for it, really. I remember you saying so. I remember you slept with Oriana's photograph over your bed, as if to steer your dreams.

Are you really ready to leave that all behind you? Are you really ready to let those dreams—your truest and deepest—go?

Because I assure you, they will haunt you for many years behind that pretty white picket fence.

Unpack those bags. Make Miami feel like home.

Then go and find the next edge you've been waiting for.

Yours,
Suzy

CHRISTINE TODD WHITMAN
Former Governor of New Jersey and EPA Administrator

~~Trust your gut.~~ If it's telling you that this is the wrong job for you, don't do it.

THERE SEEMED to be no path to walk to the front door of former governor Christie Whitman's house in Oldwick, New Jersey, so I poked around the back, looking for her. Dogs barked. I walked through the backyard gate and called through the screen door, like a nosy neighbor. No Christie. Then, just as I was getting back into my car, I saw in the distance a tall figure in front of a big building.

Oh . . . right. The barn! Christie lives on a farm, called Pontefract, where she grew up. She was waiting in front of the barn, which houses not only some of the farm's pigs, hens, and Angus cattle, but also her office (upstairs) and a refrigerator (downstairs) from which later she extracted a dozen Pontefract eggs for me to take home.

Wearing a green V-neck shirt and pants, Christie had a quiet, friendly, but reserved manner as she led me up to the roomy office in her barn. Raised by politically active parents who took her to her first national convention at age nine, Christie migrated toward government and politics early, working first for Donald Rumsfeld in the Office of Economic Opportunity and then, in 1969, at the Republican National Committee.

"I was enthusiastic, had a lot of ideas, and was willing to take on new challenges. I always doubted that I would have the capabilities but was always game to try. When you have two older brothers that's what they instill in you as you grow up," she said with a wry smile. Now her daughter, Kate, thirty-three, is following in her footsteps. In 2008, Kate placed second in a field of seven candidates when she ran for the Republican nomination for a seat in the House of Representatives.

As the first female governor of New Jersey, serving from 1994 to 2001, Christie cut taxes more than fifty times, held growth in government spending below the inflation rate, and reduced both welfare rolls and unemployment by half. She also had a huge impact on the state's environment, slashing beach closings and the number of times New Jersey violated federal air-quality rules. In fact, the Natural Resources Defense Council recognized New Jersey for instituting the most comprehensive beach-monitoring system in the nation. During her tenure, Christie also started the preservation of more than a million acres of open space and farmland, a nifty trick for a small state that lies in the congested New York City Philadelphia corridor.

Now she is president of The Whitman Strategy Group, which specializes in energy and environmental issues. She's also co-chair of the Republican Leadership Council, which supports fiscally conservative, socially tolerant candidates. Moderation and inclusion have been her political mantras ever since her rough-and-tumble years as administrator of the Environmental Protection Agency, from 2001 to 2003. She was no neophyte, of course. "Yet nothing I saw in more than fifteen years as an elected official, or in a lifetime as a participant around politics at the local, state and national levels, prepared me for what I witnessed in Washington in early 2001," she wrote in *It's My Party, Too: The Battle for the Heart of the GOP and the Future of America.*

Despite their common experience as governors (and Bush's purchase of First Dog Barney from a litter of Christie's beloved Scottish terrier, Coors), Christie and George W. Bush diverged dramatically on environmental issues. Worse, Bush often back pedaled on key positions without even consulting her.

This was painful for obvious reasons, not least because she had had serious reservations about taking the job in the first place. Tellingly, she says she never let the lease on her Washington apartment extend for longer than a month. Of her decision to accept the EPA appointment she says, "It's hard to turn down the opportunity to effect change on the national stage, but I should have stayed as governor through the end of 2001." Now sixty-three, Christie writes to herself when she was fifty-four in the fall of 2000, after Dick Cheney called to offer her the job.

Dear Christie,

Your interest in politics has always been focused on leading change. A regulatory position, in which you simply enforce rules, won't satisfy you. A cabinet position is what you'd prefer—but that's not what is being offered.

So, you have to decide. Will you continue as governor for another year—six months of which you will be a lame duck? Or will you step up into a national arena, even if it's not in an official cabinet position?

It's difficult when a president-elect asks you to do something to say "no." But that's what you should do now. Trust your gut. If it's telling you that this is the wrong job for you, don't do it. The worst problems you have gotten yourself into happened when you ignored the inner voice that was telling you what to do.

You have pretty good instincts. Let them work for you. Every time you've trusted them you haven't been sorry. Remember one week after you became governor, when your campaign was accused of offering bribes to African American ministers and black mayors? Your instincts led you to express your outrage to the press and reach out to the Reverend Jesse Jackson and the Reverend Al Sharpton, who were prepared to lead a demonstration against you. Your instincts allowed you to turn the tide while awaiting proof that the accusations were false.

Frankly, that inner wisdom knows things it's impossible for your brain to understand. About the future, for example. There's going to be a big impediment to accomplishing what you want at the EPA. And even though you only have six productive months left in the governor's office, there's going to be a cataclysmic event in 2001 that will make you wish you were there, rather than at the EPA, for the last six months of your term.

Sincerely,
Christie

Afterword

When I created *What I Know Now: Letters To My Younger Self*, the first book in this series, I hoped my readers and I would learn from the life experience of other women. Without question we did, gaining knowledge of the most intimate sort that softened some of the rough patches in our own lives.

What I did not expect was how many other benefits would radiate out of the concept of writing a letter to your younger self. Readers and audiences are comforted and inspired by the travails and wisdom revealed in the letters. Letter-writers find the process cathartic and sometimes healing. Women who create their letters in a group discover a deep well of acceptance and validation when they share them with each other.

These experiences have led me to expand upon my original idea. I've been fortunate to be invited to conduct Letters To My Younger Self Seminars for many corporations' women's leadership programs, in which a few of the company's top women create and share their letters with other women in the organization. For teams and groups wanting to develop a deeper bond, I've enjoyed leading Letters To My Younger Self Workshops, in which I guide an entire audience through the letter creation process.

I look forward to the next steps in this journey and hope you will give yourself this experience in one form or another. Please visit me at www.letterstomyyoungerself.com or contact me at info@letterstomyyoungerself.com.

All the best,
Ellyn

Acknowledgments

With enormous gratitude I'd like to thank the many hidden forces behind *What I Know Now About Success.*

To the women in the book who shared a part of their inner story, thank you for your generosity. To Trish McEvoy, particularly, you helped this book in a way that no one else could have.

My assistants, Sam Peitler and Sangeetha Subramanian, were essential sources of initiative, enthusiasm and perseverance. I'm grateful to Kellie Probst and Joanna Jordan at Central Talent Booking and Stacy Morrison at *Redbook* for forging the way in reaching out to contributors.

Thanks to my family, particularly my husband, John Witty, for their patient counsel and continuing encouragement. As always, Dottie Serdenis, Ouidad, Cathryn Mitchell and Katie Bliss never failed to offer good advice. In her inimitable style, Sally Booth provided a key introduction.

I appreciate the patience and good faith shown by my editors at Da Capo Press, Wendy Francis and Renee Sedliar, and my agent Debra Goldstein. Many thanks to the Da Capo team tending to this manuscript: Erica Truxler, Marco Pavia, Kate Burke and Kevin Hanover.

A small army of publicists, PR folks, assistants, managers and lawyers smoothed the way for my meetings and telephone appointments with the women in this book. I thank you: Jaclyn Shor, Emese Szenasy, Manda Wargo, Richard Charnoff, Don Aslan, Dan Quinn, Kelly Eggers, Dallas Sowers, Carol Payne, Tricia Kenney, Sylvia Laniado, Steve Carlis, Rebecca Gibson, Pam Stevens, Charlotte Scroggins, Cassie Aimar, Dana Muldrow, Bob Rosone, Cindy Hoppe, Christine Pietz, Sandi Mendelson, Kristin Bouton, Megan Burke, Julie Lorigan, Min Fan, Samantha Bailye, Laeticia Reid, Gail Abrahamsen, Gretchen Barra, Alexis Rodriguez, Stacey Jones, and Stacey Brann.

The *What I Know Now* book series has connected me in ways I never expected to a world of wonderful women readers, corporate executives, retreat leaders and audiences. I am most grateful for their support.

Photo Credits

Cathie Black
President of Hearst Magazines
Credit: Timothy Greenfield-Sanders

Bobbi Brown
Founder of Bobbi Brown Cosmetics
Courtesy of Bobbi Brown/personal collection

Barbara Corcoran
Real Estate Entrepreneur and Shark Tank judge
Courtesy of Barbara Corcoran/personal collection

Pamela Craig
CFO of Accenture
Courtesy of Pamela Craig/personal collection

Paula Deen
Cookbook Author and Food Network Star
Courtesy of Paula Deen/personal collection

Nance Dicciani
Former President and CEO of Specialty Materials,
a Honeywell Division
Courtesy of Nance Dicianni/personal collection

Yue-Sai Kan
Chinese American Entrepreneur and TV Personality
Courtesy of Yue-Sai Kan

Kitty Kolding
CEO of House Party
Courtesy of Kitty Kolding

Emily Kwok
Brazilian Jiu-Jitsu World Champion
Credit: Lauren Elle

Liz Lange
Founder Liz Lange Maternity
Courtesy of Liz Lange/personal collection

Emily Mann
Playwright and Artistic Director of McCarter Theater
Courtesy of Emily Mann/personal collection

Trish McEvoy
Makeup Artist and Founder Trish McEvoy
Credit: Michel Arnaud

Soledad O'Brien
CNN Anchor and Special Correspondent
Courtesy of CNN

Suze Orman
Personal Finance Author, Columnist and PBS Star
Courtesy of Suze Orman/personal collection

Ouidad
Curly Hair Entrepreneur and Founder of Ouidad
Courtesy of Ouidad/personal collection

Sylvie Rochette
Founder and CEO of Victorian Epicure
Courtesy of Sylvie Rochette/personal collection

Suzanne Somers
Actress
Credit: Ron Galella

Kate Spade
Designer and Founder of Kate Spade
Credit: Noe Dewitt

Lisa Stone
Co-Founder of BlogHer
Courtesy of Lisa Stone/personal collection

Coach Vivian Stringer
Rutgers Women's Basketball Coach
Courtesy of C. Vivian Stringer/personal collection

Suzy Welch
Author and Columnist
Credit: Eve Wetlaufer

By Pryde Brown Photographs

ELLYN SPRAGINS wrote the "Love & Money" column in the *New York Times* for three years. She now encourages women to share their wisdom through her What I Know Now™ series, seminars, and products. She lives in Pennington, New Jersey, with her family.